PRAISE FOR *COMMANDO DAD: BASIC TRAINING:*

"One of the best parenting books I've ever read"
Lorraine Kelly

"brilliant book"
The Daily Telegraph

"The advice, approved by healthcare professionals, is quick to read, easy
to understand and simple to digest, delivered in short, unambiguous
bullet points and, no-nonsense rules – and, pretty unarguably, spot on"
Jon Henley, *The Guardian*

"A no-nonsense guide to being an elite dad or carer,
from birth to three years – great package"
The Bookseller

"A must-have for new dads"
MADE Magazine

"Neil Sinclair experienced many life and death situations during his
six years as an Army Commando. But forget tracking drug traffickers
through the jungles of Belize or clearing mines in Iraq while dodging
sniper fire – the most daunting thing the dad of three has ever
faced is bringing his newborn son Samuel home from hospital"
Baby & Me magazine

COMMANDO DAD: THE COOKBOOK

An Hachette UK Company
www.hachette.co.uk

Vie Books, an imprint of Summersdale Publishers Ltd
Part of Octopus Publishing Group Limited
Carmelite House
50 Victoria Embankment
LONDON
EC4Y 0DZ
UK

www.summersdale.com

Printed and bound in China

ISBN: 978-1-78783-285-5

Substantial discounts on bulk quantities of Summersdale books are available to corporations, professional associations and other organizations. For details contact general enquiries: telephone: +44 (0) 1243 771107 or email: enquiries@summersdale.com

COMMANDO
DAD
THE COOKBOOK

EASY RECIPES FOR BUSY DADS

NEIL SINCLAIR

vie

DEDICATION

To Tara, Sam, Jude and Liberty. Long may we continue to sit around the table together – laughing, discussing, debating, supporting… and eating. And to Mum and Dad: thank you for all the good times around our dinner table. What a great start you gave us all.

DISCLAIMER

I have been a stay-at-home dad since 1 April 2003 and estimate in this time I have prepared approximately 16,000 meals for my unit. That's a lot of practice. In this book, I share recipes which have been reviewed and approved by a nutritionist. However, the publisher, authors and experts disclaim any liability from any injury that may result from the use, proper or improper, of the information contained in this book. I have suggested tasks that your trooper may help you with for each recipe, but only you can judge if your trooper will be able to undertake those tasks safely. *Commando Dad: The Cookbook* should not be considered a substitute for the advice of your healthcare professional or your own common sense.

CONTENTS

INTRODUCTION

TO EVERY MAN WHO WANTS TO PREPARE HEALTHY, NUTRITIOUS FOOD FOR THEIR UNIT (Henceforth known as "Commando Dads"): this book has been written for YOU.

This is a practical cookbook for use in the field. The recipes are straightforward, require no special skills and represent good value for money. In fact, in some instances, you won't need to cook, merely assemble well. Yet the result will be tasty and nutritious food that the whole unit will enjoy.

And enjoying good food is important. You cannot underestimate the benefits of a good diet, which include optimum growth and development, energy, better sleep, improved immunity to common illnesses and a more positive outlook. Troopers learn by example and will mimic your behaviour. Want them to eat the right amount of healthy nutritious food? Then you need to do the same. Don't worry if your diet leaves a little to be desired: it is never too early to start building good eating habits for your troopers, or too late to start improving your own.

Once the food has been prepared, where possible, aim to sit down as a unit and enjoy it together. After all, mealtimes are not only about food, but also socializing and enjoying each other's company. This relays the message, loud and clear, that not only is eating something pleasurable but that you all belong to a secure and loving unit.

It will also enable you to demonstrate what good table manners are. It is too easy to rush food, especially with so many tasks to complete. Stop!

Do:

- Teach your troopers – and yourself – to slow down and enjoy food. It takes around 20 minutes after you've started eating for the stomach to tell the brain that it is full. If you're racing your food, you won't pick up those messages, and as your troopers are following you, neither will they. If you don't give yourself time to feel full, you risk overeating.

- Praise good eating habits and table manners. Your troopers will love the attention and will repeat the behaviour to get the same response.

Don't:

- Adopt the "Do as I say, but not as I do" approach to eating. If your troopers don't see you eating well, it's unlikely they will eat well in the long term.
- Put your troopers in a position where they rush their food and consequently overeat from an early age. This can cause serious problems for troopers in the long term.

The preferred choice of drink at mealtimes is water. Make it the "norm". When the body is thirsty it requires water. Juice is high in sugar and should be limited. If juice is offered, ensure it is diluted one part juice to ten parts water.

It doesn't matter if you are responsible for feeding the whole unit every night or just occasionally, whether you are a complete novice or a seasoned cook looking for ideas. What matters is that you roll up your sleeves and get in the cookhouse with your troopers.

The Importance of Portion Sizes and a Balanced Diet

Portion size is critically important. A major cause of the obesity epidemic is that we have forgotten what a healthy portion size is, both for adults and troopers. The list below shows the main food groups with examples of their health benefits.

The Food Groups:

1. Bread, cereals and potatoes: These starchy foods, which also include pasta and rice, provide energy, fibre, vitamins and minerals.

2. Fruit and vegetables: Provide fibre, vitamins and minerals and are a source of antioxidants.

3. Milk and dairy foods – and vegan alternatives: Provide calcium for healthy bones and teeth, protein for growth, plus vitamins and minerals.

④ Meat, fish, poultry, eggs, nuts and legumes: These foods provide protein, vitamins and minerals, especially iron. Legumes also contain fibre.

⑤ Fats: Oils, dairy products, lean meats and oily fish are all good sources of fat-providing energy, omega 3 and vitamins A, D and E. Troopers up to the age of two years should be given full-fat products and not low-fat versions.

Note that processed foods, such as biscuits, cakes, fizzy drinks, chocolate, sweets, crisps and pastries, do not fit into these groups. They contain high sugar and saturated fat levels and provide empty calories with no valuable nutrition. You know that these foods aren't good choices. Limit them.

COMMANDO DAD TOP TIP

Never overfill your trooper's plate and bribe them to eat it. A trooper should only ever eat to fulfil hunger, not to please you. It is better to put too little on the plate and let your trooper tell you when they want more.

Variety is the spice of life and these tips will help you prevent food boredom.

Do:

- Help your trooper to discover different foods that will become new favourites. The more foods they try, the less likely they are to become picky eaters.

- Try to cook a completely new meal at least once a month. It can be fun to try new and interesting foods together.

Don't:

- Fall into a rut of preparing the same few meals – easy to do when you find out your trooper's "favourites".

- Feel you have to prepare a menu of new foods every week. It can be as simple as changing vegetables from carrots to sweetcorn, or replacing apples with pears, or giving oatcakes instead of bread and butter.

Lucky seven: Troopers need to be exposed to a new food at least seven times before they can form an opinion about liking it – or not. Do not give up on healthy, nutritious foods too quickly. And never ever give up trying a healthy food before the seventh time because you don't like it. Eat it seven times yourself. You may be surprised.

How to Use This Book

Unless stated otherwise, all recipes in this book are designed to feed two adults and two children. I have a family of five but as my children are now all teenagers, I double these amounts. See Chapter 2: Base-Camp Recipes for ideas on what to do with the leftovers if you cook too much.

Of course, if you double the recipes, you need to allow a little longer to cook – both for the preparation of the ingredients and the cooking. Similarly, if you're just cooking for yourself and one trooper, the cooking time will be shorter. It's best to use the original cooking times here as your reference point and monitor your food closely for the desired results.

I tend not to use too much spice in my cooking, preferring instead to have chilli flakes or sauce as a condiment on the table (primarily for my sons, who love heat). If you want to add spice while cooking, go ahead! In fact, that goes for every recipe in this book – use it as a basis to build your own recipes; swap and add ingredients to make it a favourite for your unit.

As a Commando Dad is a hands-on dad, every recipe in this book details tasks that your troopers may be able to help with. Your trooper will be thrilled to help you – cooking with you will not only help them gain confidence in their own abilities but also develop a sense of self-reliance. If that weren't enough, troopers are much more likely to try a new food they have helped prepare.

As you introduce your troopers to cooking, you will need to start with simple activities, supervise them very closely and leave enough time. You will always need more time than you think. The timings included in this book are for you cooking the meal alone, so the first time you cook it with your troops, double the suggested time – and see how you get on.

Only you can judge the tasks which are suitable for your trooper. In the next chapter, in Cookhouse Missions (see page 19), you'll find some kitchen basics that you can take them through – and a Mission Accomplished section to record when they've mastered them.

But even after they've got the basics sorted, still expect spills and slip-ups. These are inevitable and there is no point in literally crying over spilt milk. If you and your troops have worked together and have an edible meal at the end of it, you have accomplished your mission. Long after you have forgotten the cleaning up you will remember the fun you had cooking together.

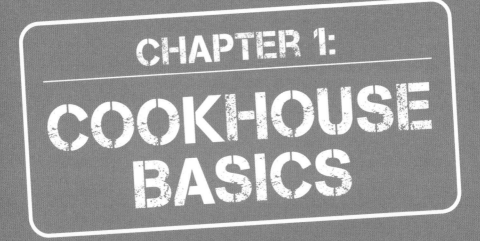

CHAPTER 1:

COOKHOUSE BASICS

CALL TO THE STORES

To prepare the recipes in this book you will need the following equipment:

- Butter knife
- Chopping board
- Colander
- Electric whisk
- Food processor
- Sharp kitchen knives
- Grater
- Hand whisk
- Juicer
- Ladle
- Masher
- Measuring jug
- Measuring spoons
- Meat thermometer
- Non-stick frying pan

- Oven gloves
- Ovenproof dish
- Pans with lids
- Pastry brush
- Peeler
- Plastic knife (to practise cutting soft food)
- Ramekins
- Scales
- Sieve
- Slotted spoon
- Spatula (fish slice)
- Springform cake tin
- Steamer

SAFETY IN THE COOKHOUSE

There is no substitute for your close supervision and you must under no circumstances leave your troopers alone during cooking. If you need to leave the cookhouse, get your troopers out too, and take pans off the heat or turn them down.

General Safety

The cookhouse is a potentially dangerous environment. To make sure you and your troopers stay safe:

Do:

1. Wash your hands in warm soapy water before and after handling food (especially meat, fish, eggs and vegetables). Give them a proper wash – it should take at least ten seconds. See instructions in Cookhouse Missions (see page 19).

2. Dress for the job: Aprons keep clothes clean, tie back long hair, don't wear loose clothing, roll up loose sleeves, and protect your feet with sensible footwear.

3. Turn pot handles inward toward the back of the hob to avoid them being heated or knocked over.

4. Open lids away from you (to avoid steam burns).

5. Clean up spills and broken glass/crockery immediately.

6. Turn everything off when you've finished cooking.

Don't:

1. Leave a trooper alone in the cookhouse when cooking is in progress.

2. Leave pans on the hob unattended.

3. Touch any electrical appliance or socket if your hands are wet.

4. Add water to a pan full of hot oil, as it may spit.

5. Leave tea towels and cloths near the cooker, hob or toaster in case they catch fire.

6. Put knives or other sharp objects into a sink full of water where they can't be seen.

7. Sneeze – but if you can't help it, turn away from the food and sneeze into the crook of your arm.

8. Stand on anything other than a sturdy footstool to reach high cupboards (keep everything you use often in easy reach).

Safe Food Handling

Safe food handling is essential to help prevent food poisoning.

Always:

- Refrigerate or freeze raw meat, fish and dairy products – they spoil quickly.

- Clean any area raw meat and/or its juices may have touched: The sink, the kitchen counter, the chopping board, utensils, etc. You don't need to use antibacterial sprays; hot, soapy water is fine.

- Put cooked food on a clean plate.

- Use separate chopping boards for raw meat, raw fish, and vegetables.

- Wash dishcloths and tea towels and dry them completely before you use them again. Dirty, damp cloths are the perfect breeding ground for germs.

Never:

- Wash raw meat – it's the high temperature of cooking that kills harmful bacteria; by washing meat the bacteria are splashed around your cookhouse.

- Leave foods unrefrigerated for longer than 2 hours at any time after preparation.

- Eat food past its use by date (which is different to its sell by date) as these dates are based on scientific tests of how quickly harmful germs can develop in the packaged food.

- Lick your fingers or put them in your mouth when handling raw food, such as meat, fish or eggs.

First Aid Kit

Every cookhouse should have a fully stocked first aid kit. A list of first aid kit items is widely available online and all lists of recommended items are similar. See for example: www.nhs.uk/common-health-questions/accidents-first-aid-and-treatments/what-should-i-keep-in-my-first-aid-kit/.

Smoke Alarm

About half of all household fires start in the kitchen. A working smoke alarm (that conforms to British Standard BS EN 14604 and ideally also carries the British Standard Kitemark) is an essential piece of safety equipment for your cookhouse. If you're reading this outside the UK, please refer to your country-specific safety recommendations.

To keep your smoke alarm in good working order, you should:

- Test it once a month, by pressing the test button until the alarm sounds.

- Clean it once every three months with your vacuum cleaner (with the soft brush attachment) to remove dust or insects.

- Change the battery once a year (unless it's a unit with a ten-year battery).

- Replace the whole unit every ten years.

It's also important to keep your oven, hob, cooker hood, extractor fan and grill clean – built-up fat and grease can ignite and cause a fire.

Take a look at your local fire and rescue service website for basic and common sense precautions to prevent fire. You can even book a home fire safety visit if you would benefit.

CRACKING THE CODE

When learning any new skill, the first obstacle to overcome is understanding unfamiliar terms.

Boil: Large bubbles quickly rise to the surface and there is constant steam.

Simmer: Smaller bubbles constantly rise to the surface with occasional wisps of steam.

Baste: Keep meat moist during cooking by spooning fat or juices over it.

Preheat: Turning the oven on and giving it time to reach the required temperature before you use it – 15 minutes should be enough, although older ovens may need 5 minutes longer.

Caramelize: Cook foods that contain sugar, such as onions, until they go brown and develop the nutty, sweet flavour of caramel.

Spot the Difference
Bicarbonate of soda and baking powder

- Bicarbonate of soda (or baking soda), when mixed with certain wet ingredients (such as milk), creates carbon dioxide – which causes your batter to rise.

- Baking powder contains bicarbonate of soda but also other ingredients, which means you need only add water for the same reaction.

Self-raising and plain flour

Self-raising flour is simply plain flour with baking powder added. This means that if you buy plain flour, you can make it self-raising when the recipe calls for it. This is a smart move in my opinion, as it reduces waste. As a rule of thumb, I put 2 teaspoons of baking powder for every 200 g of plain flour.

Sauté and stir-fry

If there is a difference, I haven't worked it out yet. It basically amounts to cooking vegetables quickly in very hot oil so that they maintain their colour, crunch and vitamins.

Sell by and use by

It's not always necessary to throw food out if it's past its best before date; it's about quality and does not mean the food is unsafe. If it looks and smells bad, it's been left too long. Use by dates should be adhered to.

Substitutes

There's always going to come a time when you need something for a recipe that you don't have. Usually at the last minute. Before you go back to the shops and waste time and money, make sure you don't already have something that you could use as a substitute. For example, half a mashed avocado instead of an egg works in baking, or Greek yoghurt instead of sour cream, or vinegar instead of lemon juice (use half the amount!). Just do a quick search on the internet "what can I use instead of...?" Do use it as an opportunity to experiment with different flavours too – you may even create your own dish! A lot of work has gone into producing the food that's already in your cupboards – eat and enjoy it. Handy substitutes include:

- To substitute baking powder in a recipe, add 1 teaspoon of bicarbonate of soda to the dry ingredients for every 3 teaspoons of baking powder the recipe calls for.

- Lemon juice for vinegar: If you're all out of vinegar, substitute with lemon juice; the acidity of the lemon mimics that of the vinegar.

- Oats or crushed cornflakes for breadcrumbs.

- Avocado or apple purée for egg (in baking).

- Maple syrup or agave syrup for honey.

Weights and Measures

It's handy to know Cookhouse Conversions, especially in baking, where measurement does need to be accurate. I haven't included conversions for the American "cup" measurement here because they differ between wet and dry ingredients.

Weights

Imperial	Metric
½ oz	10 g
¾ oz	20 g
1 oz	25 g
2 oz	50 g
3 oz	75 g
1 lb	450 g
1 lb 8 oz	700 g
2 lb	900 g
3 lb	1.35 kg

Volume

Imperial	Metric
Teaspoon (tsp, t)	5 ml
Tablespoon (tbsp, T)	15 ml
2 fl. oz	75 ml
5 fl. oz (¼ pint)	150 ml
10 fl. oz (½ pint)	275 ml
1 pint	570 ml
1¼ pints	725 ml
1¾ pints	1 litre
2 pints	1.2 litres

Temperature

Gas Mark	Celsius	Fahrenheit	Temperature
1	140	275	cool
2	150	300	cool
3	170	325	warm
4	180	350	moderate
5	190	375	moderate
6	200	400	moderate/hot
7	220	425	hot
8	230	450	hot
9	245	475	hot
10	260	500	very hot

COOKHOUSE MISSIONS

Throughout this book I list some basic kitchen tasks that your troops can help you with. However, basic does not always mean simple, especially if you've never performed the task before. Cookhouse Missions are the key skills that your troops need to master to help you with any recipe in this book (always starting with washing hands!). Before you attempt a recipe, check if your trooper has mastered the basic skills they need to help. If not, follow the guidance on pages 20–45.

COMMON SENSE

- As you introduce your troopers to cooking, supervise them very closely and leave enough time. It is going to get messy – embrace it. And remember that, when it comes to safety, there is no substitute for your close supervision.

WASHING HANDS

Mission brief

- **Kit list:** Running water (warm or cold), soap – alcohol-based handwash can be used if no soap is available – and a clean, dry towel (used only for drying hands).
- **Mission notes:** An essential first step for everyone engaged on a cookhouse sortie.

INSTRUCTIONS:

1. Wet hands and turn off the tap.

2. Apply the soap and loosen up those vocal chords – hand washing takes 20 seconds (long enough for you and the troops to sing the alphabet song).

3. Clean your palms: Rub hands together.

4. Clean the back of your hands and sides of fingers: Rub the back of one hand with the palm of the other, fingers intertwined – making sure that you soap and clean in between your fingers. Repeat with the opposite hand.

5. Clean the front of your hands and fingers: Rub your hands together with your fingers intertwined.

6. Clean the back of your fingers: Rub the backs of your fingers against your palms with fingers interlocked.

7. Clean your thumbs: Wrap one hand around the opposite thumb and rotate that opposite hand to ensure the thumb is clean all round. Repeat with the other hand.

8. Clean the tips of your fingers: Rub the tips of your fingers in the opposite palm in a circular motion, going backward and forward. Repeat with the other hand.

9. Turn on the tap and rinse your hands thoroughly.

10. Turn off the tap with the corner of your towel.

11. Dry hands.

MISSION ACCOMPLISHED

I verify that on this date .... I learned to wash my hands properly with my Commando Dad.

Signed...

WASHING FRUIT AND VEGETABLES

Mission brief

- **Kit list:** Cool water, dedicated scrubbing brush (I use a nail brush kept only for this purpose as it's easy to hold), bowl of clean water and a colander to put washed fruit and veg in.
- **Mission notes:** Washing fruit and vegetables will remove dirt and protect you from foodborne illnesses.

INSTRUCTIONS:

1. Wash and dry your hands.

2. Gently wash vegetables and fruit, using your common sense. Some, such as lettuce and berries, for example, can be put into a colander and rinsed gently with water. Others, such as muddy leeks or radishes, for example, can be rubbed gently under a running tap. Only vegetables with thick skins and a lot of dirt – such as potatoes or carrots – should be scrubbed in a bowl of water.

3. Put clean produce in a colander, give it a final rinse and then leave it to drain until needed.

4. Wash and dry your hands.

MISSION ACCOMPLISHED

I verify that on this date .... I learned to wash fruit and vegetables properly with my Commando Dad.

Signed...

MISSION:

PEELING

Mission brief

- **Kit list:** A peeler that is easy for your trooper to grip, equipment for cleaning fruit and veg, if needed, and a clean chopping board (ideally used only for vegetables).
- **Mission notes:** Golden rules of peeling vegetables are to always peel away from you and not to press too hard (or you'll start to lose the flesh, too).

INSTRUCTIONS:

1. Wash and dry your hands.

2. Wash the fruit and veg.

3. If peeling long vegetables (such as carrots or parsnips):
   - Put the tip of the vegetable on the chopping board and start peeling halfway down.
   - Use downward strokes, and turn the vegetable to make sure you peel all the way around.
   - When it is half peeled, turn it upside down and repeat.

4. If peeling round fruit and vegetables (such as apples or potatoes) make sure your trooper can comfortably clasp the item in one hand, so it can be held securely while peeling.

5. Use small downward strokes, turning the fruit or vegetable to make sure it is peeled all the way around.

6. Wash and dry your hands.

MISSION ACCOMPLISHED

I verify that on this date .... I learned to peel fruit and vegetables properly with my Commando Dad.

Signed..

Please note: One of the recipes in this book will require you to peel ginger – you peel that simply by scraping the skin away gently with a spoon!

GRATING

> ## Mission brief
> - **Kit list:** A box grater, equipment for washing and peeling food, if needed, and a clean chopping board.
> - **Mission notes:** Graters are sharp and can easily cut small fingers. Don't let troopers press food too hard against the grater, always grate away from you and leave a chunk of food to hold onto to avoid grating fingers.

INSTRUCTIONS:

1. Wash and dry your hands.

2. Put your box grater on the chopping board. You'll need the hand you write with to hold the food you're grating, so use the other hand to hold the grater by its handle at the top.

3. Take your food (making sure it's washed and peeled if needed) and then grate from top to bottom. Don't ever grate both ways, and keep your fingers away from the grating edge.

4. Tap the grater with a spoon to dislodge all the food within the grater.

5. Take the food off the chopping board and, if it's not being used straight away, put it in a bowl or tub, cover it, and put it in the fridge.

6. Wash and dry your hands.

MISSION ACCOMPLISHED

I verify that on this date .... I learned to grate properly with my Commando Dad.

Signed...

CUTTING

Mission brief

- **Kit list:** Equipment for cleaning fruit and veg, if needed, a clean chopping board and a sharp and appropriately sized knife. You can buy knives specifically for troopers or use a smaller adult one. Blunt knives don't cut through easily, encouraging troopers to use force to cut – by pressing harder. This can cause the blade to bounce or slide off the food.
- **Mission notes:** To prepare your troopers for cutting, they can practise by cutting soft ingredients with a plastic knife – such as butter or mushrooms. When you're comfortable for them to proceed to a knife, there are two safe methods to learn, both of which keep their fingers away from the knife blade.
  - The bridge (good for cutting food into segments).
  - The claw (good for slicing and dicing).

GOLDEN RULES FOR TROOPERS USING KNIVES

- Never let troopers hold the food they're cutting in their hand. It should always be cut on a chopping board.
- Make sure your chopping board is stable and secure.
- Always hold the knife carefully.
- Always cut away from you.
- If your hand is wet and feels slippery, stop and dry your hands.
- Never move around the kitchen with a knife in your hand.

- Never drop a sharp knife into the washing-up bowl, always leave it at the side of the sink where it can be seen and washed carefully.
- Always wash and dry your hands after touching raw food.

INSTRUCTIONS FOR THE BRIDGE METHOD:

A good food to practise this technique on is tomatoes (not cherry tomatoes which may put little fingers too near the knife for beginners). Tomatoes are the right size to hold and let the trooper focus all their concentration on their knife skills.

1. Wash and dry your hands.
2. Put the tomato on the clean chopping board.
3. You'll be cutting with the hand you write with, so put your other hand on the tomato near where you are going to make the cut.

4 Make a bridge over the tomato with your hand, by putting your fingers on one side and your thumb on the other. The space between your hand and the food will look like a bridge. Make sure the space between your hand and the tomato is large enough to cut safely.

5 Take the knife in your other hand and make sure that the blade is facing downward.

6 Guide the knife under the bridge and using that forward motion, cut the tomato down the middle.

7 Keeping the knife in the tomato, pull the knife out of the bridge.

8 Repeat.

9 When the tomato has been cut in half, put down the knife.

10 Place the tomato half flat-side down and cut it in the same way.

11 Repeat until the tomato is in four segments.

12 When all cutting is complete, put the knife next to the sink where it can be easily seen and washed carefully.

13 Wash and dry your hands.

MISSION ACCOMPLISHED

I verify that on this date .... I learned how to use the bridge method for cutting with my Commando Dad.

Signed...

INSTRUCTIONS FOR THE CLAW METHOD:

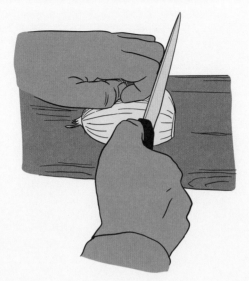

This method will protect fingers and is a key knife skill to take into adulthood. A good food to practise this technique on is celery, as the ridges make it easier for your trooper to grip.

1. Wash and dry your hands.

2. Wash the celery if it is dirty and put it on the clean chopping board (your Commando Dad might want to take the top and bottom of the celery stick off for you).

3. You'll be cutting with the hand you write with, so put your other hand on the celery near where you are going to make the cut.

4. Make a claw by gripping the food stuff with the tips of your fingers and then lean your fingers slightly forward. When you look down at your hand you shouldn't be able to see your nails, although the tips of your fingers are holding the celery tightly.

⑤ Keep your thumbs tucked in.

⑥ Pick up the knife with your writing hand and make sure the blade is pointing downward.

⑦ Place the blade of the knife onto the celery, in line with the straight part of your fingers, and keep your fingertips tucked in.

⑧ Slice through the celery carefully.

⑨ Move your fingers back and slice through the celery again.

⑩ Repeat until you have enough slices.

⑪ When all slicing is complete, put the knife next to the sink where it can be easily seen and washed carefully.

⑫ Wash and dry your hands.

MISSION ACCOMPLISHED

I verify that on this date .... I learned how to use the claw method for cutting with my Commando Dad.

Signed...

MEASURING

Mission brief

- **Kit list:** Scales (digital ones are more accurate), clean teaspoon and tablespoon, clean measuring jug that can measure litres and millilitres, not pints.
- **Mission notes:** Throughout this book I use grams, millilitres, teaspoons and tablespoons. Find out how to measure these on pages 34–35.

INSTRUCTIONS FOR MEASURING WITH SCALES:

Scales are typically used for measuring dry ingredients.

1. Wash and dry your hands.

2. Put your scales on a stable, flat surface.

3. Put a clean plate or bowl onto the scales before turning them on (if they're digital) so that it reads "0", or adjust the dial to "0" if your scales are manual.

4. Make sure that you have the correct unit of measurement (kilograms and grams – or kg and g – for the purposes of this book).

5. Tip the food you're measuring onto the clean plate or bowl.

6. If you're tipping something heavy (like a bag of flour for example) you may find it easier to use a spoon instead.

7. If you're measuring several things, always make sure you set the scales back to zero, after putting the clean plate or bowl on them.

INSTRUCTIONS FOR MEASURING WITH A JUG:

Measuring jugs are used for measuring liquid.

1. Wash and dry your hands.

2. Take a clean measuring jug and set it on a stable surface.

3. Make sure that you have the correct unit of measurement (litres and millilitres – or l and ml – for the purposes of this book).

4. Pour the liquid.

5. Lean down so that the jug is at eye level to check if you have the correct amount – the liquid should come directly to the line – not above or below it.

INSTRUCTIONS FOR MEASURING WITH TABLESPOONS AND TEASPOONS:

Typically used for measuring small amounts of dry products, such as herbs, spices, sugar and salt – but can also be used when smaller amounts of liquid ingredients (such as oil) are required.

1. Wash and dry your hands.

2. Take a clean and dry measuring spoon (a teaspoon – tsp or t – and tablespoon – tbsp or T).

3. Take a clean bowl to measure over (that way if any extra ingredients fall off the spoon they don't fall onto your counter top, and can be put back in their packaging).

4. For dry ingredients: Scoop the ingredients into the spoon and gently scrape off the excess with the straight edge of a table or butter knife. You don't need to scrape off the excess if the recipe says the spoon can be "heaped".

5. For sticky ingredients, like honey, you may wish to warm the measuring spoon first. Ask your Commando Dad to leave the spoon to rest in a cup of hot water for about 30 seconds and then the sticky liquid will slide off the spoon easily.

MISSION ACCOMPLISHED

I verify that on this date .... I learned how to measure food properly with my Commando Dad.

Signed..

MIXING

Mission brief

- **Kit list:** A large clean bowl, a spoon, fork or hand whisk, and the ingredients you need to mix.
- **Mission notes:** Mixing just means combining two or more ingredients lightly together. Usually you mix wet and dry ingredients separately before bringing them together.

INSTRUCTIONS:

1. Wash and dry your hands.

2. Tip the ingredients to be mixed into a large clean bowl.

3. Gently mix them together – be careful not to spill the ingredients over the edge of the bowl.

MISSION ACCOMPLISHED

I verify that on this date .... I learned how to mix food properly with my Commando Dad.

Signed..

SIFTING

> ## Mission brief
> - **Kit list:** A large clean bowl, a sieve.
> - **Mission notes:** Sifting breaks up any lumps in the flour, adds air and makes it easier to mix into other ingredients when forming a cake batter or making dough.

INSTRUCTIONS:

1. Wash and dry your hands.

2. Hold your sieve over the bowl.

3. Put the ingredients that need to be sifted into the sieve (don't overload it though as it may be too heavy; spoon the ingredients in so that the weight is comfortable for you).

4. Holding the sieve over the bowl with the hand you write with, gently tap the sieve against the palm of the opposite hand (don't just shake the sieve as this can get messy).

5. The higher you can hold the sieve, the lighter the sifted ingredients will be (but be careful not to spill them over the sides of your bowl).

MISSION ACCOMPLISHED

I verify that on this date .... I learned how to sift properly with my Commando Dad.

Signed...

MISSION:

MASHING

Mission brief

- **Kit list:** A large clean bowl, a fork or potato masher.
- **Mission notes:** Mashing can be done with a fork (for mashing soft food such as avocados and bananas) or a potato masher for potatoes and other vegetables.

INSTRUCTIONS:

1. Wash and dry your hands.

2. If mashing with a fork, place your foodstuff in the bowl and press gently with a fork. Don't overdo it as you may turn it into a purée (a creamy liquid).

3. If mashing potatoes or other vegetables, you will probably be mashing them in the cooking pot, which can be hot, so be careful.

4. Make sure the pot is on a stable surface and press down on the potatoes using the masher.

5. Once you've broken up the potatoes you can add the other ingredients (such as butter and milk) and repeat the process until the potatoes are smooth and mashed well.

MISSION ACCOMPLISHED

I verify that on this date .... I learned how to mash properly with my Commando Dad.

Signed...

MISSION:

KNEADING

> ## Mission brief
> - **Kit list:** Dough (see jam tarts recipe on page 194 for ingredients), a clean work surface, flour for dusting, a butter knife.
> - **Mission notes:** Kneading is used in making dough and is used to mix the ingredients and add strength to the final food.

INSTRUCTIONS:

1. Wash and dry your hands.

2. Sprinkle your work surface with flour.

3. Put the dough on your work surface – it may be sticky and this is fine.

4. Grasp the side of the dough furthest away from you and fold it in half toward you.

5. Then use the heels of both of your hands and the weight of your body to push the dough into itself.

6. Turn the dough – if it has stuck to the work surface, use a butter knife to gently release the dough and sprinkle a little more flour onto the work surface and the dough, if needed. Just be careful not to use too much flour – kneading will reduce stickiness – as this will ruin the recipe.

7. Repeat the process (fold, press and turn) until the dough is smooth and elastic.

8. Wash and dry your hands.

MISSION ACCOMPLISHED

I verify that on this date .... I learned how to knead food properly with my Commando Dad.

Signed..

BEATING

Mission brief

- **Kit list:** A large clean bowl, a fork or hand whisk, and the ingredients you want to beat.
- **Mission notes:** Beating is a more vigorous form of mixing, because the purpose is not only to combine ingredients but also to get air into the mixture.

INSTRUCTIONS:

1 Wash and dry your hands.

2 Tip the ingredients to be beaten into a large clean bowl.

3 If you can, tip the bowl slightly on edge away from you and whisk using a circular motion. This will bring as much air as possible into the baking ingredients.

MISSION ACCOMPLISHED

I verify that on this date .... I learned how to beat properly with my Commando Dad.

Signed...

TAKING THE TEMPERATURE OF MEAT

Mission brief

- **Kit list:** A meat thermometer, oven gloves.
- **Mission notes:** You can't tell if meat is safely cooked by sight, smell or even taste. A food thermometer is the only way to ensure meat is cooked and that any harmful bacteria have been killed.

INSTRUCTIONS:

1. Wash and dry your hands.

2. Remove meat from the oven or take off the heat.

3. Ensure your meat is on a stable surface – use oven gloves to protect your hands, if it is still in its hot cooking tray.

4. Push the meat thermometer into the thickest part of the meat to get an accurate reading – and be careful not to touch bone, fat or gristle.

5. Wash the thermometer in hot, soapy water straight away (after each use).

6. Repeat until the meat has reached the required temperature.

MISSION ACCOMPLISHED

I verify that on this date .... I learned how to take the temperature of meat properly with my Commando Dad.

Signed...

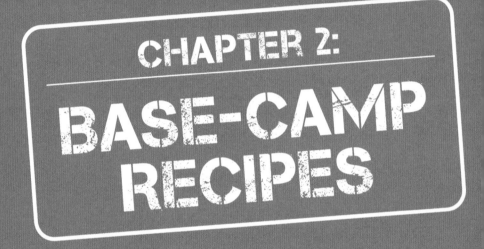

CHAPTER 2:

BASE-CAMP RECIPES

SHOP – AND EAT – SMART TO SAVE MONEY AND REDUCE WASTE

Before we jump into recipes, I want to take a few moments to talk to you about the importance of shopping well, eating what you buy and reducing food waste.

According to Friends of the Earth, every single year Brits throw away over 10 million tonnes of food. The average UK family spends £470 a year on food that they bin plus the proportion of their council tax spent on disposing of that perfectly edible "waste". And this is in a country where 8.4 million people are struggling to afford to eat.

And the problem is not just limited to the UK. Approximately 100 million tonnes of food are thrown away in the EU every year, and the Food and Agriculture Organization (FAO) of the United Nations estimates that 1.3 billion tonnes of food is wasted globally each year. This represents one third of all food produced for human consumption.

Reducing food waste is easier than you think and is based on the principle of just buying what you need – and using as much of it as possible. Here are some tips to help you:

- Make a meal plan for the week that uses some of the same key ingredients. For example, a whole chicken can be used to make roast chicken, chicken salad and a soup. Before you dismiss this as being too boring, look at your eating habits now. This approach will save time in shopping, thinking of what to cook and food preparation.

- Make a list of the food that you need for your meal plan. But before you go shopping, check what you have already. Really look – even in the backs of those cupboards with tins and deep down in the drawers of your freezer. You could be surprised.

- Stick to your list. This is key to buying only what you need. Supermarkets aren't there to feed us, they exist to sell us food, and they're good at it. Tempting offers, delicious smells, expensive products at eye level – ignore them all. A two-for-one offer on something you don't need doesn't represent a 50 per cent saving so much as a 100 per cent waste of your money.

- Try to do one big shop (meaning one dedicated time to buy everything – not necessarily buying from one shop). If you limit the amount of times you need to pop to the shop to get groceries, you will limit the amount of times you're tempted to make impulse purchases. It's that simple. And don't ever – ever – do your big shop while you're hungry because you'll buy more. I have the battle scars to prove it.

- Shop at smaller local shops such as greengrocers, butchers, bakers, local farmers selling eggs and vegetables, etc. You are more likely to be able to buy just what you need, fresh, in season with fewer miles from "field to fork" and less packaging. And you even get the warm feeling that comes with supporting your local community.

- Know how to substitute one ingredient for another (so you can use what you already have where possible – see Substitutes on page 16).

- Make friends with your freezer. The freezer is a great tool to reduce food waste because it keeps everything fresh until you need it. Every year, approximately one third of all the food produced for human consumption across the world gets lost or wasted. Take bread for instance – one of the most commonly wasted foodstuffs in the world – in the UK and Germany 900,000 and 1.7 million tonnes respectively are thrown away. Yet fresh bread kept in the freezer can be used as needed (it defrosts quickly at room temperature or can be popped straight into the toaster!) and stale bread makes excellent breadcrumbs for freezing. Leftover filter coffee can be frozen in ice-cube trays and used in iced coffee. Other staples such as milk, butter and herbs can be frozen meaning that you'll never run out. Do some research to find out how your freezer could work harder for you.

- Know what to do with leftovers. Despite all your best efforts, leftovers are inevitable. Before you scrape them into the bin, see if you can use them to make another meal. Excess rice can make a rice pudding, for example, and vegetables can be used in everything from soup to samosas. What about leftover foods that haven't been cooked? Do a quick internet search for other recipes – there'll be lots to try. If fresh fruit is overripe, use it straight away or freeze it (for example, peeled bananas cut into coin sizes can be used to make excellent smoothies).

- Don't throw things out because they've reached their best before date (use by dates are another matter – see Spot the Difference on page 16 for more information).

Don't forget to compost scraps of fruit and vegetables to avoid them ending up in landfill where they cannot decompose naturally.

GOLDEN RULES

For each recipe I have included a Mission Brief, which includes:

- The kit you'll need.
- The skills needed (so you can decide whether your troopers can help).
- An indication of time and cost, and how many servings.
- Ingredients.
- Instructions.

THE BASICS

The following recipes are basics that are not only very easy and quick to pull together but can also be used as the basis for other meals. For example, your basic tomato sauce can be used on its own with pasta (it's good with grated cheese on top), or perhaps spiced up (chilli flakes should do it) and served with meatballs, or you might want to add some oregano and use it to make a lasagne. On the odd occasion I've had leftovers, I've even had it the next day on a sausage sandwich (it works, trust me).

The options are endless. But first you must master the basics.

BASIC TOMATO SAUCE

Mission brief

- **Kit:** Pan (I use a frying pan, but depending on how much you're making you may need a saucepan), knife, chopping board, garlic press (you can chop the garlic if you prefer), spoon for stirring (ideally one with a silicone or wooden handle to reduce the chance of burns), can opener.
- **Skills:** Opening cans, peeling, chopping, using a garlic press, stirring a pan (hot).

TIME NEEDED: 30 MINUTES • SERVES: 4 • COST: £ £ £ £ £

INGREDIENTS:

- 2 tbsp cooking oil
- 1 small onion, finely chopped
- 2 garlic cloves, chopped or put through a press
- 2 x 400 g tins chopped tomatoes
- Herbs and spices if you want to use them. How much you use will depend on how much you like them but never less than a teaspoon for a herb or half a teaspoon for spice

- is a good rule of thumb. You can always use more (or less!) next time you cook it. For a traditional tomato sauce try adding "mixed herbs" (easily found sold dried in jars)
- Knob of butter (to make the sauce glossy and rich)
- Splash of balsamic vinegar (optional – but it does give the sauce a depth of flavour and doesn't taste vinegary)

INSTRUCTIONS:

1. Add the oil to the pan and heat on a low to medium heat.

2 Gently fry the onion until soft and translucent, about 5–7 minutes – don't let it start to go brown.

3 Add the garlic and fry for a further 2 minutes.

4 Add the tomatoes and any herbs or spices you're using.

5 Stir well.

6 Turn up the heat until the mixture is bubbling, and then reduce it to a simmer so that the sauce can thicken.

7 Stir it every few minutes to make sure it's not sticking to the pan or cooking too fast.

8 When the sauce is at your desired consistency, take it off the heat. Don't cook for less than 10 minutes, but a thick sauce can take up to 40 minutes.

9 Stir in a knob of butter and balsamic vinegar if using.

10 Put a lid on to keep it warm until you're ready to serve.

TIP: If the heat is too high when the sauce is reducing it will spit out of the pan. Think of lava flow. If this is the case, get the troops well back, reduce the heat and wipe up the mess before it sets. Don't be tempted to put a lid on as your sauce won't be able to thicken.

BASIC WHITE SAUCE

Mission brief

- **Kit:** Saucepan, measuring jug and spoons, whisk – a silicone handle will reduce the chance of the whisk becoming too hot.
- **Skills:** Measuring, whisking a sauce (hot).
- **Mission notes:** A white sauce – or béchamel – is the foundation of many savoury sauces. You can use it to make cheese sauce (which you can mix with veggies and serve with pasta, or make a cauliflower cheese, for example), or a parsley sauce, which is great with fish or ham. You can also use it in lasagne and as a pie filling. I don't use the traditional method of making a "roux" (basically cooking fat and flour together and adding milk gradually) because I personally find it fiddly and time consuming – this sauce is quick, easy and lump-free every time.

TIME NEEDED: 15 MINUTES • SERVES: 4–6 AS A SAUCE; OR USE TO MAKE A WHOLE PIE/LASAGNE • COST: £ £ £ £ £

INGREDIENTS:

- 500 ml milk
- 50 g plain flour
- 50 g butter
- Salt and pepper

INSTRUCTIONS:

1. Put the milk, flour and butter into a saucepan and heat on a medium heat.

2. Whisk continuously (gently at first), until the sauce has thickened (5 minutes).

③ Dip a teaspoon in and let it cool before tasting. If you can taste flour, keep going.

④ When it's reached the desired thickness, take off the heat.

⑤ Add salt and pepper.

⑥ Add your flavourings (see below) if using and stir in, and serve.

For recipes in this book that use this recipe, see:

Cauliflower cheese – page 145
Lasagne – page 80
Mac 'n' cheese – page 82

VARIATIONS

Cheese sauce:

100 g cheese, which you'll need to add gradually and keep stirring in until melted. Mature Cheddar gives a great flavour for this sauce, but I tend to supplement it with any spare cheese I have (Parmesan, feta, mozzarella, etc.) and it's especially good for frozen cheese, which goes crumbly when defrosted. I freeze spare cheese for this purpose.

Parsley sauce:

4–5 heaped tbsp fresh parsley, 1 tbsp dried parsley or 2 tbsp frozen parsley. Gently stir the herb into the sauce.

BASIC SOUP

SERVE WITH: Bread, crackers or, if you have the time, you might want to make croutons (which are a tasty addition to salads and stews and a great way to use up stale bread. They therefore qualify for inclusion in the basics section – see page 57).

Mission brief

- **Kit:** Saucepan, measuring jug, peeler, ladle, chopping board and knife, electric blender.
- **Skills:** Measuring, peeling, chopping, using a blender (noisy but ever popular).
- **Mission notes:** I am a big fan of soup because it gives a new lease of life to any spare veg that's knocking about in your fridge and can make a tasty and nutritious meal in minutes.

TIME NEEDED: 30 MINUTES • SERVES: 4 • COST: £ £ £ £ £

INGREDIENTS:

- 1 tbsp cooking oil
- 250 g vegetables of your choice, chopped. Good choices include celery, carrots, onion, parsnip, leeks – but I literally use any raw veg I have
- 250 g potatoes, peeled and chopped
- 700 ml vegetable stock (3–4 stock cubes added to boiling water)
- Seasoning to taste (salt and pepper)

INSTRUCTIONS:

1. Add oil to pan and put on a medium heat.
2. Add all vegetables and fry gently for 3–5 minutes, or until they begin to soften.

③ Add stock and simmer gently for 15 minutes, or until the vegetables are tender.

④ Remove from the heat and allow to cool.

⑤ Taste to see if your soup requires any seasoning.

⑥ Ladle into a blender and blend until smooth.

⑦ Return to the pan and gently reheat on a medium heat for 3–5 minutes and serve.

TIP: Always taste your soup before seasoning as you may have enough salt from the stock.

VARIATIONS:

- A more hearty soup:
  - Add 50 g of rinsed red lentils at the same time as the stock, but you'll need to add 250 ml of extra water (not stock – just water) to cook them.
  - Add an extra potato. The more potatoes, the thicker the soup.
  - Add any cooked rice you have to the blended soup.

- A more tomatoey soup: Reduce the amount of stock to 400 ml and add one x 400 g can of chopped tomatoes.

- A more herby or spicy soup: You can add a teaspoon of herbs and spices while frying your vegetables. Smoked paprika, curry powder, cumin, basil or mixed herbs have all worked well for my unit. If everyone eating it likes heat, you could add ¼ tsp cayenne pepper or chilli flakes (if only a few of you like heat, you might want to put a chilli mill on the table).

BASIC CROUTONS

Mission brief

- **Kit:** Bread knife, wooden spoon, baking tray, big bowl (for mixing), oven gloves.
- **Skills:** Cutting bread, stirring.

TIME NEEDED: 20 MINUTES • SERVES: 4 • COST: £££££

INGREDIENTS:

- 4 thick slices of bread – slightly stale bread is perfect
- ¼ tsp garlic powder
- ¼ tsp salt
- 4 tbsp olive oil or rapeseed oil

INSTRUCTIONS:

1. Preheat the oven to 190°C.

2. Slice the bread into roughly equal sizes.

3. Put the bread, garlic powder and salt in the big bowl and stir with the wooden spoon.

4. Tip the olive oil in a little at a time, gently tossing the bread until it's all absorbed.

5. Spread the bread into an even layer on a baking tray (no need to oil).

6. Bake for 10 minutes, or until golden brown and crisp and serve.

TIP: If you have lots of slightly stale bread that needs to be used up, make a big batch of croutons and seal them in a plastic sandwich bag, pressing out all of the air before freezing. Defrost them whenever you want to add them to salads, stews or soup.

BASIC CRUMBLE

SERVE WITH: Custard, cream, ice cream, yoghurt.

Mission brief

- **Kit:** Mixing bowl and spoon, measuring scales and spoons.
- **Skills:** Mixing, rubbing.
- **Mission notes:** Bake a delicious fruit crumble. If you can make a crumble, you'll never be without a quick and easy fruit pudding. This is particularly useful in the summer months when fruit is plentiful and cheap, or in autumn with seasonal apples.

TIME NEEDED: 10 MINUTES • SERVES: 5 • COST: £ £ £ £ £

INGREDIENTS:

- 200 g plain flour
- 110 g golden caster sugar
- ¼ tsp salt
- 110 g cold butter, cubed

INSTRUCTIONS:

1. Put flour, golden caster sugar and salt in a bowl and mix.

2. Add butter to bowl and rub it in until the mixture looks like breadcrumbs.

TIP: "Rubbing" (lightly rubbing the ingredients between fingers and thumbs) will prevent the mixture clumping and becoming pastry dough.

3 This is now ready to be added to prepared fruit (see variations) and baked in a preheated oven at 190°C for 30 minutes, or until the top is golden, and served.

VARIATIONS:

- Apple crumble: Peel, core and slice three large cooking apples (approx. 300 g), mix in 2 tbsp caster sugar and 1 tsp cinnamon. Arrange in a baking dish so there are no holes (for the crumble to fall through) before sprinkling the crumble on top and baking.

- Frozen fruit crumble: Put 1 kg frozen berries into a saucepan with 50 g sugar and heat gently until the fruit is soft and all the sugar has dissolved. Pour into a baking dish and wait for it to cool for 10 minutes at least before sprinkling the crumble on top and baking.

- Rhubarb crumble: Cut ten sticks (approx. 1 kg) rhubarb into cubes, place on a baking tray and sprinkle with 4 tbsp of water and 2 tbsp of caster sugar. Bake for 10 minutes, then put in the baking dish. Sprinkle with 1 tsp ground ginger and mix well before adding the crumble and baking.

⚠ WARNING:

The crumble will be super-hot when it comes out of the oven. Do not be tempted to taste it too quickly.

BASIC BISCUITS

Mission brief

- **Kit**: Big mixing bowl, a sieve for sifting, wooden spoon, cling film, spatula, baking tray, wire rack, measuring scales, oven gloves.
- **Skills**: Measuring, creaming, beating, sifting, rolling biscuit dough into balls.

TIME NEEDED: 30 MINUTES • MAKES: 35 BISCUITS • COST: £ £ £ £ £

INGREDIENTS:

- 225 g butter, softened (plus a little for greasing your baking tray)
- 110 g caster sugar
- 275 g plain flour
- See Variations on page 62 in case you need extra ingredients

INSTRUCTIONS:

1. Preheat oven to 180°C.
2. Grease your baking tray.
3. Put the butter and sugar into the mixing bowl. Cream (that is, beat together) until the mixture becomes smooth in texture and pale yellow in colour.
4. Sift the flour into the bowl and mix well until combined into a dough.
5. Using your hands, take a small amount of the dough (approx. the size of a cherry) and roll into a ball.
6. Place each ball onto the baking tray making sure to leave 4–5 cm of space between them.
7. Press down gently on each ball.
8. Put in the oven to bake for 15 minutes until the biscuits are light-golden brown.

(9) Remove from oven and allow to cool for 2 minutes before using your spatula to carefully put the biscuits onto the wire rack. Let the biscuits cool before you taste them, to avoid burns.

TIP: If you don't want to cook all 35 biscuits at once, you can save the mixture for later by storing it in the fridge for up to five days or in the freezer for up to four months. To do this, put a large sheet of cling film on your work surface and put your remaining biscuit dough onto it.

Make a sausage shape quickly (avoid touching the dough too much) and wrap the cling film around it tightly. Twist the ends so that it looks like a cracker.

Put it in the fridge or freezer until you're ready to use.

When using straight out of the freezer, you don't need to roll the dough. Just slice biscuits straight off the dough sausage and pop them onto the greased baking tray.

VARIATIONS:

- Chocolate chip biscuits: Mix 125 g chocolate chips into the dough.

- Chocolate biscuits: Sift 250 g flour and 50 g cocoa powder for your dough.

- Spice biscuits: Add 1 tsp cinnamon or mixed spice to the flour when sifting.

- Orange biscuits: Add 1 tsp orange essence to your butter and sugar before you add the sifted flour (if you also use cocoa as above, you'll have chocolate orange biscuits).

- Vanilla biscuits: Add 1 tsp vanilla essence to your butter and sugar before you add the sifted flour.

BASIC SPONGE CAKE

Mission brief

- **Kit:** A big mixing bowl, two non-stick 18-cm round cake tins, a sieve for sifting, an electric whisk or wooden spoon, wire rack for cooling, skewer, oven gloves, measuring scales.
- **Skills:** Using an electric whisk or mixing with a wooden spoon, using a skewer, sifting, measuring.

TIME NEEDED: 1 HOUR • SERVES: 8 • COST: £ £ £ £ £

INGREDIENTS:

- 225 g self-raising flour
- 1 tsp baking powder
- 225 g caster sugar
- 4 eggs
- 225 g butter (softened)
- Your filling, see page 64

INSTRUCTIONS:

1. Preheat oven to 180°C.

2. Put the dry ingredients (flour, baking powder and sugar) in your large mixing bowl and make a "well" in the middle.

3. Put your wet ingredients (eggs and butter) into the well.

4. Whisk with an electric whisk – starting at a low speed until everything is combined – and then switching to a higher speed until the mixture is light and fluffy. Alternatively, beat the mixture with a wooden spoon until it reaches the same consistency.

5. Pour the mixture into the two baking tins.

6 Put in the centre of the oven for 20–25 minutes, or until they are golden brown.

7 Test they're done by putting a skewer into the centre of each. It needs to come out clean; if there's any raw cake mixture on the skewer, it needs to be cooked longer.

8 Once the cakes are out of the oven, let them cool for 10 minutes before tipping them on the rack to cool completely and serve.

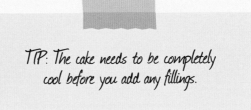

TIP: The cake needs to be completely cool before you add any fillings.

FILLINGS:

I don't specify amounts here apart from the buttercream (see recipe on the facing page) – add to taste.

- Jam
- Lemon curd
- Jam and buttercream
- Jam and chocolate buttercream

BASIC BUTTERCREAM

Mission brief

- **Kit:** Big bowl (for mixing), big sieve (for sifting), measuring scales and spoons, wooden spoon.
- **Skills:** Measuring, sifting, beating, spreading.

TIME NEEDED: 10 MINS • SERVES: FILLS ONE CAKE • COST: £ £ £ £ £

INGREDIENTS:

- 140 g butter, at room temperature (it needs to be soft)
- 280 g icing sugar (sifted)
- 1–2 tbsp water or milk

INSTRUCTIONS:

1. Put the softened butter and half your icing sugar into the bowl and beat until smooth.
2. Add the rest of the icing sugar and 1 tbsp water or milk and beat until creamy.
3. If the mixture is too stiff, add the other tbsp of water.
4. Fill cake with buttercream and serve.

TIP: If you forgot to take your butter out of the fridge, don't put it in the microwave to soften; you'll start to cook it. Instead, cut it into cubes, place into your bowl and beat it until soft.

MEALS IN MINUTES

Every Commando Dad needs to have a few recipes that he can rustle up in minutes, for those inevitable days when timings go awry.

If you don't have any leftovers you can repurpose, you could make a sandwich or beans on toast (neither of which you need a recipe for). However, I also wanted to give you some recipes for surprisingly quick meals.

You may also want to look at the Breakfasts recipes for other suitable ideas – see page 148.

BAKED HAM AND EGGS

SERVE WITH: Toast cut into strips, or soldiers, for dipping.

Mission brief

- **Kit:** Ramekin, grater, toaster.
- **Skills:** Greasing, cracking eggs.

TIME NEEDED: 25 MINUTES • SERVES: 1 • COST: £ £ £ £ £

INGREDIENTS:

- Butter/oil to grease the ramekin and butter the toast
- 1 slice ham
- 1 egg
- 10 g cheese, grated

INSTRUCTIONS:

1. Preheat the oven to 180°C.

2. Grease the ramekin and put the ham in – you're aiming to line the ramekin and create a cup shape. It doesn't have to be perfect – you may have some ham poking out the top of the ramekin for example, and this is fine.

3. Crack the egg straight onto the top of the ham – no need to beat.

4. Cover with cheese.

5. Bake in the oven for 12–15 minutes.

6. Let it cool slightly and serve with toast. You may want to scoop the contents onto a plate to stop little fingers being burned. The ham "cup" makes this an easy process.

CROQUE-MONSIEUR

Mission brief
- **Kit:** Grater, frying pan, baking tray, spatula.
- **Skills:** Grating, buttering.

TIME NEEDED: 20 MINUTES • SERVES: 2 • COST: £ £ £ £ £

INGREDIENTS:

- 4 slices bread (wholemeal bread works well)
- 2 tsp Dijon mustard
- 80 g cheese, grated
- 2 slices ham
- 30 g butter

INSTRUCTIONS:

1. Preheat the oven to 180°C.

2. Spread ½ tsp mustard over each slice of bread.

3. Add half of the grated cheese, a slice of ham, and the rest of the cheese and the other slice of bread.

4. Sandwich the two pieces of bread together and press down firmly. Repeat this process to create the second sandwich.

5. Heat butter in a large frying pan until sizzling.

6. Place the sandwiches into the pan then fry both sides of the sandwiches for 1–2 minutes. Use a spatula and a fork to carefully turn the sandwiches over; each side should be golden brown in colour.

7. Transfer sandwiches to a baking tray and place in the oven for 4–5 minutes, until cheese has melted.

8 Remove from oven, slice each sandwich in half and leave to cool for a few minutes and serve.

TIP: Melted cheese is incredibly hot so if you are faced with hungry, impatient troopers, it may help to cut the sandwich into smaller squares to aid cooling.

OMELETTE

Mission brief
- **Kit:** Mixing bowl, whisk, spatula.
- **Skills:** Whisking, flipping.

TIME NEEDED: 5 MINUTES • SERVES: 1 • COST: £ £ £ £ £

INGREDIENTS:

- 2–3 eggs
- 25 g butter
- Optional extra: Pinch of mixed herbs
- Seasoning to taste (salt and pepper)

INSTRUCTIONS:

1. Beat the eggs together in a mixing bowl.

2. Add the herbs and seasoning, if using.

3. Melt the butter in a frying pan until foaming, but not brown.

4. Pour in the eggs and swirl the pan until the pan surface is covered.

5. As soon as the eggs start to cook (you'll know as they'll start to set), lift up one edge of the omelette with a spatula, tilt the pan and let the uncooked egg run underneath.

6. Continue to do this until the omelette is ready – this will be when the middle is slightly liquid but the rest is firm. If you cook until the centre is firm, your omelette may be dry.

7. Flip it in half (this will finish cooking the slightly liquid centre) and serve.

VARIATIONS:

- Cheese and tomato: Prepare as above, but add 50 g grated cheese and one chopped tomato to the eggs before pouring into the frying pan.
- Bacon: Cut two rashers of bacon into little pieces and fry for a couple of minutes, then add to the egg mixture and follow the instructions above.

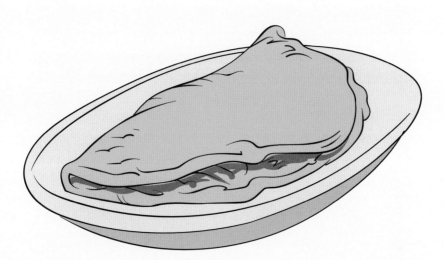

PRAWN STIR-FRY

Mission brief

- **Kit:** Grater, wok or big pan, peeler.
- **Skills:** Grating, stirring, chopping, peeling.
- **Mission notes:** Stir-fry takes just a few minutes to cook so the secret is to have everything prepared before you start cooking.

TIME NEEDED: 25 MINUTES • SERVES: 4 • COST: £ £ £ £ £

INGREDIENTS:

- 200 g dried egg noodles
- 1 tbsp cooking oil
- 1 garlic clove, sliced
- 1 cm fresh ginger, peeled and grated
- 500 g vegetables, such as peppers, carrots, baby corn, mange tout, broccoli, cabbage or pak choi – cut them into roughly equal sizes so they cook at the same rate
- 1½ tbsp soy sauce
- 200 g cooked prawns

INSTRUCTIONS:

1. Cook the noodles according to the packet instructions, drain and set aside.

2. Heat the oil in a large frying pan or wok, then fry the garlic and ginger for 1 minute, stirring well.

3. Add the veg and stir to make sure they are coated.

4. Fry for 2–3 minutes then add the soy sauce and mix well.

5. Cook for 2–3 minutes more until the veg are tender.

6 Add the cooked noodles and stir.

7 Add the prawns, stir through and make sure all ingredients are hot, and serve.

TIP: Have a good look for spare veg you have in your fridge as stir-fry is a great way to give them a new lease of life. Even spare salad leaves (not the bitter ones) can be used.

VARIATIONS:

This stir-fry works well with other cooked meats too – such as shredded chicken, pork or flaked fish – making it a great recipe for leftovers.

PRAWN SCAMPI

SERVE WITH: Parmesan cheese, a squeeze of lemon juice and fresh parsley, if using.

Mission brief

- **Kit:** Chopping board and knife, garlic press (optional), wok or large saucepan.
- **Skills:** Mincing/chopping garlic, slicing lemon, measuring.
- **Mission notes:** This is not battered fish but prawns cooked in butter and served with pasta. It's simple and delicious, and you can easily change the portion sizes to suit your troopers' tastes.

TIME NEEDED: 30 MINUTES • SERVES: 4 • COST: £ £ £ £ £

INGREDIENTS:

- 200 g pasta of your choice
- 3 cloves garlic, minced or sliced
- 75 ml fish stock or white wine, if you have any
- 2 tbsp olive oil
- 500 g prawns, fresh or frozen (defrosted)
- 45 g butter
- 85 g Parmesan cheese, grated
- Seasoning to taste (salt and pepper)
- 1 lemon, cut into quarters and fresh parsley to serve on top, if you choose

INSTRUCTIONS:

1. Put your pasta in a pan of boiling water according to packet instructions and leave to cook while you make the sauce.

2. Prepare garlic and stock (or wine).

3. Heat olive oil and garlic over a medium heat for 2 minutes.

4. Add prawns and cook for 2 minutes.

5. Add about a third of the butter and all the stock or wine.

6. Cook for about 2 more minutes. Remove from heat.

7. Drain cooked pasta and add to the prawns.

8. Add the remaining butter and stir through gently.

9. Season as required and serve with Parmesan cheese, lemon juice and parsley (if using).

THE CLASSICS

You can't beat the Classics.

These recipes are all hearty crowd pleasers, perfect for when you can get the unit around the table.

TOAD IN THE HOLE

SERVE WITH: Peas or freshly steamed green vegetables.

Mission brief

- **Kit:** Measuring scales, jug and spoons, mixing bowl, whisk, ovenproof dish, oven gloves.
- **Skills:** Mixing, beating, measuring.

TIME NEEDED: 45 MINUTES • SERVES: 4 • COST: £ £ £ £ £

INGREDIENTS:

- 100 g plain flour
- Pinch of salt
- 1 egg
- 250 ml milk
- 500 g good quality sausages
- 3 tbsp cooking oil

INSTRUCTIONS:

1. Preheat the oven to 200°C.
2. Place the flour and a pinch of salt in the bowl.
3. Make a well and break the egg into it.
4. Add a little milk and mix together until smooth.
5. Pour in the rest of the milk and beat for a minute or so to form a batter.
6. Put the sausages in an ovenproof dish with the oil, and bake for 10 minutes.
7. Remove the dish from the oven and pour in the batter.
8. Return to the oven and cook for a further 25 minutes or until the batter has risen and is browned, and serve.

FISH CAKES

SERVE WITH: Vegetables, salad.

Mission brief

- **Kit:** Peeler, chopping board and knife, potato masher, measuring scales, jug and spoons, frying pan, mixing bowl, three shallow bowls, whisk, spatula, wooden spoon, two large plates, kitchen roll.
- **Skills:** Peeling, chopping, measuring, slicing, mixing, mashing, frying.

**TIME NEEDED: 1 HOUR 30 MINUTES •
SERVES: MAKES 12 SMALL FISHCAKES • COST: £ £ £ £ £**

INGREDIENTS:

- 3 large potatoes, peeled and chopped
- 20 g butter (for mash)
- 400 g fresh or frozen filleted fish – cod, coley, salmon, pollock, hake, haddock, for example
- 250 ml milk
- 4 spring onions, sliced
- Optional: 1 tbsp fresh dill or 1 tsp dried dill
- 6 tbsp cooking oil (3 tbsp for binding and 3 tbsp for frying)
- Salt and pepper to taste
- 3 tbsp plain flour
- 2 eggs
- 125 g breadcrumbs (you can make your own by blitzing any bread you have that's going stale)

INSTRUCTIONS:

1. Place the potatoes in the saucepan, cover with cold water and put them on the heat to boil. Reduce the heat to a simmer and cook them until they're so soft they slide off a fork (about 15 minutes).

2. Drain the potatoes, mash with the butter and set aside in a mixing bowl to cool.

3. Cut the fish into evenly sized pieces, removing any bones you find.

4. Place the milk and fish in a shallow frying pan and gently simmer on a low heat until the fish is opaque.

5. In the meantime, place the spring onions in the bowl with the potato (and dill, if using).

6. Remove the fish from the pan and place on a plate to cool before flaking it into the potato mix.

7. Add 3 tbsp of oil and seasoning, if desired, before mixing until everything is thoroughly combined.

8. Using your hands, divide ingredients into 12 equal-sized fish cake patties.

9. Add 3 tbsp of flour in a bowl and set aside.

10. Break the eggs into a separate bowl, whisk lightly and set aside.

11. Add the breadcrumbs in a separate bowl and set aside.

12. Take each individual fishcake, dip it in the flour, dust off any excess, dip it into the egg, then fully coat in breadcrumbs before placing them on a large plate.

13. Heat oil in a frying pan on a medium heat and add fishcakes. Don't "crowd" the pan.

14. Fry each fishcake for 10 minutes, turning regularly until each side is browned.

15. Remove from heat, place on the other large plate with kitchen roll before serving.

LASAGNE

SERVE WITH: A mixed salad: shredded lettuce, cubed cucumber, cherry tomatoes and garlic bread (see page 141 for recipe).

Mission brief

- **Kit:** Chopping board and knife, measuring scales and spoons, can opener, garlic press (if mincing), wooden spoon, saucepan, shallow ovenproof dish, oven gloves.
- **Skills:** Peeling, chopping onions, opening cans, measuring, greasing.

**TIME NEEDED: 1 HOUR 30 MINUTES •
SERVES: 4 (GENEROUS PORTIONS) • COST: £££££**

INGREDIENTS:

- 2 tbsp cooking oil
- 1 large onion, chopped
- 2 cloves garlic, minced or chopped
- 500 g minced beef
- 1 x 400 g can chopped tomatoes
- 2 tsp oregano (or mixed herbs)
- 125 ml beef stock
- 2 tbsp tomato purée
- Seasoning to taste (salt and pepper)
- 6 lasagne sheets
- Cheese sauce (see page 54)
- 60 g Cheddar or mozzarella cheese, grated, for the top

INSTRUCTIONS:

1 Preheat oven to 200°C.

2 Heat the oil in a saucepan on a medium heat, add the onion and garlic and gently fry for 5 minutes.

3 Add the mince and cook thoroughly, stirring occasionally to avoid clumps forming.

4 Add the tomatoes, oregano, beef stock, tomato purée and seasoning and bring to the boil. Reduce the heat and simmer for 15–20 minutes.

5 While the meat sauce is reducing, prepare the cheese sauce (see cheese sauce recipe on page 54).

6 Grease an ovenproof baking dish then make the lasagne:
- Layer of meat sauce.
- Layer of lasagne sheets.
- Layer of cheese sauce.
- Repeat until all your ingredients have gone – ensuring you end with cheese sauce.
- Sprinkle grated cheese on top.

7 Bake for 30–40 minutes, until the top is lightly browned, and serve.

MAC 'N' CHEESE

Mission brief

- **Kit:** Two saucepans, colander, whisk, grater, measuring scales and spoons, deep ovenproof dish.
- **Skills:** Beating, measuring.

TIME NEEDED: 45 MINUTES • SERVES: 4 • COST: £ £ £ £ £

INGREDIENTS:

- 300 g dried macaroni
- White sauce (see page 53)
- 300 g grated Cheddar cheese

INSTRUCTIONS:

1. Cook the macaroni according to the packet instructions, drain and set aside.

2. Make a white sauce (see page 53).

3. Remove the pan from the heat and add about two thirds of the cheese, and stir until melted.

4. Add the macaroni to the sauce and mix well to make sure the pasta is thoroughly coated.

5. Preheat the grill.

6. Transfer the mixture to a deep ovenproof dish and sprinkle over the remaining cheese.

7. Put the dish under the grill and cook until the cheese is browned and bubbling, then serve.

CHEESE AND POTATO PIE

SERVE WITH: Vegetables or, my favourite, baked beans.

Mission brief

- **Kit:** Grater, potato peeler, chopping board and knife, big saucepan, masher, ovenproof dish, oven gloves.
- **Skills:** Peeling, chopping, grating, measuring, mashing, stirring.

TIME NEEDED: 1 HOUR • SERVES: 4 • COST: £ £ £ £ £

INGREDIENTS:

- 1.5 kg potatoes, peeled and chopped
- 1 medium onion, chopped
- 30 g butter
- 1 tbsp milk
- 175 g Cheddar cheese, grated

INSTRUCTIONS:

1. Preheat oven to 180°C.

2. Place the potatoes and onions in cold water and bring to the boil, then reduce to a simmer until potatoes are soft.

3. Drain and mash the potatoes and onion mixture with butter and milk.

4. Stir in two thirds of the cheese gradually, ensuring it is well mixed.

5. Transfer the mixture to an ovenproof dish, cover with the remaining cheese and bake until the cheese has melted and started to brown, and serve.

BANGERS AND MASH

Mission brief

- **Kit:** Chopping board, knife, peeler, lidded saucepan, colander, frying pan, masher, measuring scales and spoons, baking tin, oven gloves.
- **Skills:** Peeling, chopping, frying.
- **Mission notes:** This recipe includes an onion gravy made using gravy granules, as there are no "drippings" from cooked meat to make it with. If you'd prefer to make your gravy from scratch, see page 140 – but don't forget to factor in a little more time.

TIME NEEDED: 50 MINUTES • SERVES: 4 • COST: £ £ £ £ £

INGREDIENTS:

- 1 kg potatoes, peeled and chopped
- 8 sausages
- 1 onion, sliced
- 1½ tbsp cooking oil, plus a little extra for greasing
- 100 g butter
- 100 g milk
- Seasoning to taste (salt and pepper)
- Beef gravy granules

INSTRUCTIONS:

1. Preheat oven to 200°C.

2. Place the potatoes in a cold pan of water, bring to the boil with the lid on, remove the lid, reduce heat to a simmer and cook until soft. Then drain into a colander.

③ In the meantime, grease a baking tin, space your sausages out evenly and put them in the middle rack for 20–25 minutes, turning once.

④ Place the onion in a frying pan and fry on a low heat in cooking oil for 10 minutes until the onions start to go brown.

⑤ Using the pan the potatoes were cooked in, heat the butter and milk until the butter is melted. Turn off the heat, add the potatoes and mash (adding seasoning, if desired).

⑥ Boil the kettle and make desired amount of gravy, and add to the frying pan with the onions and heat through.

⑦ Assemble and serve.

TIP: Chopping your potatoes to a roughly equal size will ensure they will all be cooked at the same time.

TIP: I bake my sausages for convenience: No sausages spitting on the stove top and I only need to turn them once.

SPAGHETTI BOLOGNESE

Mission brief

- **Kit:** Chopping board and sharp knife, peeler, garlic press (optional), large saucepan, large frying pan.
- **Skills:** Peeling, chopping, opening cans, measuring.

TIME NEEDED: 1 HOUR 30 MINUTES • SERVES: 4 • COST: £££££

INGREDIENTS:

- 1 tbsp cooking oil
- 1 medium onion, chopped finely
- 2 cloves garlic, minced or chopped
- 1 medium carrot, chopped finely
- 1 stick celery, chopped finely
- 50 g streaky or smoked bacon, chopped
- 350 g minced beef

- 1 x 400 g can chopped tomatoes
- 2 tsp dried oregano
- 90 ml red wine, if you have any
- 2 tbsp tomato purée
- Seasoning to taste (salt and pepper)
- 350 g spaghetti or your favourite pasta

INSTRUCTIONS:

1. Heat the oil in a large frying pan, add the onion and gently fry for 3 minutes.

2. Add the garlic, carrot, celery and bacon and fry for a further 3–4 minutes.

3. Add the minced beef and cook on a high heat for a further 3 minutes until all the meat is browned.

4 Stir in the tomatoes, oregano and wine (if you are using) and bring to the boil.

5 Reduce the heat, stir in tomato purée and season to taste.

6 Leave to simmer for about 45 minutes. After about 30 minutes, put a pan of water on to boil and cook the pasta according to the packet instructions.

7 Drain your pasta, add to the Bolognese sauce, mix well, and serve.

BAKED CHICKEN WITH PARMA HAM

SERVE WITH: This dish goes well with a crunchy green salad and garlic bread, or boiled potatoes and vegetables.

Mission brief

- **Kit:** Chopping board and knife, baking tray, cling film, rolling pin, oven gloves, measuring spoons.
- **Skills:** Slicing, greasing, assembling "the sausage".

TIME NEEDED: 1 HOUR 15 MINUTES • SERVES: 4 • COST: £ £ £ £ £

INGREDIENTS:

- 1 large ball mozzarella
- 4 small chicken breasts
- Seasoning to taste (salt and pepper)
- Basil pesto (1–2 tsp per breast)
- Basil leaves (optional)
- Parma ham (3–4 slices per chicken breast)
- 1 tsp cooking oil for greasing

INSTRUCTIONS:

1. Preheat oven to 200°C.

2. Slice the mozzarella into 2-cm-wide strips and set aside.

3. Sandwich chicken breasts between two large pieces of cling film.

4. Use the rolling pin to gently pound the chicken flat, to a thickness of about 4 mm.

⑤ Remove the top layer of cling film and season the chicken breast if desired.

⑥ Spread pesto on each chicken breast.

⑦ Place the mozzarella pieces in the centre of the chicken, leaving 2 cm at each end.

⑧ Add basil leaves if using.

⑨ Take one long edge of each chicken breast and fold over the mozzarella/pesto mix then roll into a sausage shape. Squish the ends of the breast in to create a seal. The cling film can be used to help create a tight sausage.

⑩ Lay the Parma ham on a clean chopping board in horizontal, overlapping strips.

⑪ Place the chicken vertically in the centre of the strips.

⑫ Wrap the strips of ham around the chicken sausage as tightly as possible and try to fold the end in to keep the ingredients of the sausage in place.

⑬ Grease a baking tray with the oil, add the chicken and put on the top shelf of the oven.

⑭ Bake for 20–30 minutes until the ham is crisp.

⑮ Remove from the oven, set aside to rest for 10 minutes and then slice each sausage into thick, round slices and serve.

CORNED BEEF HASH

SERVE WITH: Goes well with peas, sweetcorn and green beans.

Mission brief

- **Kit:** Medium-sized frying pan, mixing bowl, potato peeler, masher, large saucepan with lid, chopping board and knife, ovenproof dish.
- **Skills:** Opening a corned beef tin, mashing, grating, chopping.
- **Mission notes:** I think this dish packs a taste punch – I don't add seasoning as I find the corned beef salty enough.

TIME NEEDED: 1 HOUR 15 MINUTES • SERVES: 4 • COST: £ £ £ £ £

INGREDIENTS:

- 400 g potatoes, peeled and chopped
- 25 g butter
- 1 medium onion, finely chopped
- 1 tbsp cooking oil
- 340 g tin of corned beef
- 75 g Cheddar cheese, grated

INSTRUCTIONS:

1. Preheat the oven to 180°C.

2. Place the potatoes in a cold pan of water, bring to the boil with the lid on, remove the lid, reduce heat to a simmer and cook until soft. Drain and mash with the butter.

3. Place the onion in a frying pan with the oil and gently fry until soft.

4 Crumble the corned beef into a mixing bowl, add the fried onion and mix well.

5 Transfer the mixture to an ovenproof dish.

6 Spread the mashed potato over the meat mixture.

7 Sprinkle the grated cheese on top, bake for 30 minutes and serve.

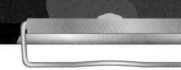

JACKET POTATOES

Mission brief

- **Kit:** Vegetable brush, small sharp knife for removing eyes and bad spots, fork.
- **Skills:** Washing potatoes, pricking a potato.
- **Mission notes:** A crispy skin, fluffy centre and a tasty filling make jacket potatoes a great meal – and although you need an hour to cook them, they are low-maintenance – just put them in the oven.

TIME NEEDED: 1 HOUR 10 MINUTES • SERVES: 4 •
COST: £ £ £ £ £

INGREDIENTS:

- 4 baking potatoes, washed and any eyes or bad spots removed
- Salt

INSTRUCTIONS:

1. Preheat the oven to 210°C.

2. Use a fork to prick your potato several times.

3. While your potato is still damp, sprinkle it with salt and rub it into the skin all over.

4. Place the potatoes directly onto the middle shelf of the oven – not touching each other – and bake for about 60 minutes.

5. Test the potato by putting a knife in the middle to see if it is soft and serve.

FILLINGS

Butter is the classic filling and great if you're serving your potato as a vegetable accompaniment to a piece of steak or chicken, for example. However, if the potato is your meal, the filling options are endless. Here's some to get you started:

- Butter and cheese.

- Baked beans and cheese.

- Mince: any leftover Bolognese sauce (see page 86 for the recipe), cottage pie filling (see page 94 for the recipe) or chilli.

- "Pizza" – a spoon of tomato sauce (recipe on page 51), mild cheese and a pepperoni slice or two. If you prefer melted cheese, you can put it in the microwave – but be sure to check it every few seconds.

- Tuna mashed in mayonnaise, sprinkled with garlic salt.

TIP: The best baking potatoes are dark brown and rough skinned, like King Edward or Maris Piper.

COTTAGE PIE

SERVE WITH: Steamed vegetables.

Mission brief
- **Kit:** Potato peeler, chopping board and knife, large frying pan, large saucepan with lid, colander, masher, ovenproof dish, oven gloves.
- **Skills:** Peeling, chopping, stirring, opening can.
- **Mission notes:** What's the difference between cottage and shepherd's pie? Cottage pie is made with minced beef and shepherd's pie is minced lamb.

TIME NEEDED: 1 HOUR 15 MINUTES • SERVES: 4 •
COST: £ £ £ £ £

INGREDIENTS:

- 1 kg non-waxy potatoes, peeled and chopped
- 50 g butter
- 1 tbsp cooking oil
- 1 medium onion, finely chopped
- 2 medium carrots, finely chopped

- 500 g lean minced beef, broken into pieces
- 1 x 400 g can chopped tomatoes
- 300 ml beef stock
- 1 tsp Worcestershire sauce

INSTRUCTIONS:

1 Preheat the oven to 190°C.

2. Place the potatoes in a pan of water, bring to the boil with the lid on, remove the lid, reduce heat to a simmer and cook until soft. Drain and mash with the butter. Put the lid back on to keep the potatoes warm.

3. Heat the oil in a large frying pan, add the onion and carrots and fry for 5 minutes until they begin to soften.

4. Add the beef and fry for a further 10 minutes until it browns, stirring occasionally to stop it sticking.

5. Pour in the tomatoes and stock. Stir well and bring to the boil.

6. Reduce the heat and simmer for 10 minutes.

7. Add the Worcestershire sauce.

8. Transfer the mixture to an ovenproof dish and evenly spread the mashed potato over the top.

9. Bake in the preheated oven for 30 minutes and serve when golden brown.

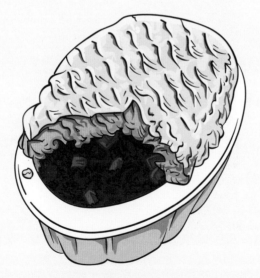

ROAST CHICKEN

Mission brief

- **Kit:** Roasting tin, chopping board and knife, ovenproof gloves, kitchen foil, meat thermometer.
- **Skills:** Cutting lemon, taking the temperature of meat.
- **Mission notes:** I love making a roast dinner; once you have the meat (or vegetarian alternative) in the oven, you are free to make the trimmings (see page 143). Whatever your roast is, remember to bring the meat up to room temperature (half an hour out of the fridge will do it) and let it rest after cooking – this will make it juicier. I haven't included how to make the vegetables here – just steam or boil as you prefer – but I have included cauliflower cheese, roast potatoes and Yorkshire puddings in the Sauces and Sides section (see page 134).
- For home-made gravy, see page 140.

TIME: COOKING TIME PLUS 15 MINUTES FOR THE CHICKEN TO REST • COST: £ £ £ £ £

INGREDIENTS:

- Chicken
- Lemon, sliced into quarters
- Garlic cloves, unpeeled

INSTRUCTIONS:

1. Preheat oven to 180°C.

2. Calculate the cooking time of the chicken: It needs to be roasted for 20 minutes per 500 g plus 10–20 minutes.

3 Put the chicken on the roasting tin, breast side down.

4 Place the lemon and garlic in the cavity of the chicken before putting it in the oven.

5 After half an hour, turn the chicken the other way up and cook for the remaining time.

6 To check if the chicken is cooked, remove from the oven and insert the meat thermometer into the thigh, but not touching bone. The safe internal temperature for a cooked chicken is 75°C.

7 When cooked, cover the chicken in foil and leave to rest in the roasting tin for 15 minutes before carving and then serve.

TIP: Cooking the chicken upside down for the first half an hour makes a juicy chicken. I don't use any other oil.

ROAST BEEF

Mission brief

- **Kit:** Roasting tin, ovenproof gloves, kitchen foil, meat thermometer.
- **Skills:** Taking the temperature of meat.

TIME: COOKING TIME PLUS 20 MINUTES FOR THE JOINT TO REST • COST: £ £ £ £ £

INGREDIENTS:

- Beef joint
- Olive oil to pour on the meat
- Seasoning to taste (salt and pepper)

INSTRUCTIONS:

1. Preheat oven to 180°C.

2. Calculate the cooking time of the beef: it needs to be roasted for 20 minutes per 500 g, plus 20 minutes (this is medium rare. For rare, cook for 15 minutes less).

3. Put the joint in a roasting tin and pour the oil over the top and the sides. Season as desired and place into the oven.

4. Baste the joint (spooning the hot juice from the pan all over the joint) three times during cooking.

5. Insert a meat thermometer into the thickest part of the joint to ensure it is cooked.

6. When the meat is cooked, wrap it in foil and leave to rest for 20 minutes before carving and then serve.

ROAST LAMB

Mission brief
- **Kit:** Roasting tin, ovenproof gloves, kitchen foil, knife.
- **Skills:** Taking the temperature of meat.

TIME: COOKING TIME PLUS 20 MINUTES FOR THE JOINT TO REST • COST: £££££

INGREDIENTS:
- Lamb joint
- Olive oil for drizzling over the meat
- Salt and pepper

INSTRUCTIONS:

1. Preheat oven to 180°C.

2. Calculate the cooking time of the lamb: it needs to be roasted for 20 minutes per 500 g, plus 20 minutes (this is medium rare. For rare, cook for 15 minutes less).

3. Put the joint in a roasting tin and drizzle the oil over the top and the sides. Season as desired and place into the oven.

4. Baste the joint (spooning the hot juice from the pan all over the joint) every 20 minutes or so during cooking.

5. Insert a meat thermometer into the thickest part of the joint to ensure it is cooked.

6. When the meat is cooked, wrap it in foil and leave to rest for 20 minutes before carving, and then serve.

ROAST PORK AND CRACKLING

Mission brief
- **Kit:** Kitchen paper, roasting tin, ovenproof gloves, kitchen foil, knife.
- **Skills:** Taking the temperature of meat.
- **Mission notes:** Crackling is crispy roast pork skin – you need to start cooking in a very hot oven to achieve this.

TIME: COOKING TIME PLUS 20 MINUTES FOR THE JOINT TO REST • COST: £ £ £ £ £

INGREDIENTS:

- Pork joint
- Olive oil to rub on the skin
- Salt and pepper

INSTRUCTIONS:

1. Preheat oven to 240°C.

2. Calculate the cooking time of the pork: It needs to be roasted for 25 minutes per 500 g plus 25 minutes.

3. Put the joint in a roasting tin and pat the skin dry with kitchen paper.

4. The skin needs to be scored evenly and you can add more cuts with a sharp knife as this will help create crunchy crackling. Cut about halfway into the skin.

5. Rub oil into the skin and add salt and pepper. It is important to rub the seasoning deep into the scored skin.

6 Place the pork on the high shelf in the oven and roast for 25 minutes.

7 Turn the heat down to 190°C and cook for the remaining time.

8 Insert a meat thermometer into the thickest part of the pork to ensure it is cooked.

9 Take out of the oven, remove crackling from the pork and place on a plate crispy side up. Cover the pork with foil and allow it to rest for at least 20 minutes – then carve, serve and enjoy.

ONE-POT WONDERS

These recipes provide delicious, filling, straightforward meals that can be made in just one pot.

As an added bonus, the stews and casseroles can be prepared in advance and then cooked over a few hours, to develop a rich flavour – and a cookhouse that smells amazing!

PESTO RISOTTO

SERVE WITH: A mixed salad: Shredded lettuce, cubed cucumber, celery, etc.

Mission brief

- **Kit:** Large pan or wok, chopping board and knife, garlic press (optional), wooden spoon.
- **Skills:** Peeling, cutting and chopping, measuring, stirring.
- **Mission notes:** Risotto needs a lot of attention, but the effort is worth it as risotto is a tasty, creamy, satisfying dish. It's very flexible too – I've included my family's favourite, but also check out my variations on page 105.

TIME NEEDED: 45 MINUTES • SERVES: 4 • COST: £ £ £ £ £

INGREDIENTS:

- 1 tbsp olive oil
- 1 medium onion, peeled and chopped
- 1 clove of garlic, chopped or minced
- 200 g Arborio rice
- 650 ml vegetable stock
- Seasoning to taste (salt and pepper)
- 120 g basil pesto
- 200 g cherry tomatoes, halved
- 25 g cheese, grated

INSTRUCTIONS:

1. Heat oil in your pan, then fry the onion and garlic on a medium heat for 3–4 minutes.

2. Add the rice to the onions and garlic and fry gently for a further minute or two.

3 Add the stock to the rice, a little at a time, stirring all the while, until the stock is absorbed. Continue until all your stock is absorbed – about 20 minutes.

4 Test the rice to see if it is tender. If it isn't, add a little hot water and repeat the process until it is ready.

5 Take off the heat and stir in pesto and cherry tomatoes.

6 Put in serving bowls and season if required.

7 Top with grated cheese and serve.

VARIATIONS:

Risotto is a versatile dish and you can add your unit's favourite ingredients as the last step. Here are a few ideas to get you started:

- Mushroom risotto: Clean, slice and fry 250 g mushrooms in 15 g of butter and set aside, complete with the cooking liquid that the mushrooms create (basically the water released from the mushrooms, together with the butter). Prepare the rice as above and when you take it off the heat, stir in the mushrooms and an extra knob of butter. Season to taste and serve.

- Sweetcorn risotto: Gently fry two large, chopped leeks and 300 g sweetcorn in 20 g of butter and set aside. Prepare the rice as above and when you take it off the heat, stir in the leeks and corn, season to taste and serve.

- Spinach and tomato risotto: When you're cooking the rice and still have about a quarter of your stock left, stir in two chopped fresh tomatoes and continue. With the last bit of stock you put in, add a pack of washed baby spinach. When all stock is absorbed, take off the heat, stir in 25 g grated Parmesan cheese until it melts, season and serve.

If you'd prefer a meat version, just add cooked meat at the last step. In fact, it's a great way to use up any leftovers you have.

BEEF CASSEROLE

SERVE WITH: Mashed potato.

Mission brief

- **Kit:** Chopping board and knife, garlic press (optional), sieve, plate, wooden spoon, ovenproof gloves, flameproof casserole dish with lid.
- **Skills:** Peeling, cutting and chopping, measuring, stirring.

TIME NEEDED: 2 HOURS 30 MINUTES • SERVES: 4 •
COST: £££££

INGREDIENTS:

- 40 g plain flour
- Seasoning to taste (salt and pepper)
- 500 g stewing steak, cut into bite-sized pieces
- 2 tbsp cooking oil
- 1 large onion, chopped
- 1 clove garlic, minced or sliced
- 500 ml beef stock
- 3 medium carrots, chopped
- 1 bay leaf

INSTRUCTIONS:

1 Preheat oven to 180°C.

2 Sift some of the flour over a plate and add seasoning.

3 Roll the prepared meat in the seasoned flour (shake off excess) and set aside.

4 Heat the oil on the hob in the casserole dish.

5. Brown the meat on all sides, remove and set aside.

6. Fry the onion and garlic for a couple of minutes in the casserole dish, add the rest of the flour to the pan and fry gently.

7. Add the stock and boil, stirring constantly to avoid lumps, until it thickens.

8. Add the carrots and meat to the dish, with the bay leaf and put the lid on.

9. Place in the oven for 90 minutes to 2 hours.

10. Remove the bay leaf before serving.

TIP: Keep an eye on your casserole. Add tomatoes and/or stock if it looks like it's drying out or, if you'd like it thicker, take the lid off for the final half hour.

SLOW COOKED LAMB

SERVE WITH: Mashed potato and vegetables of your choice.

Mission brief
- **Kit:** Chopping board and knife, ovenproof gloves, flameproof casserole dish with lid, measuring jug and spoons, spoon.
- **Skills:** Peeling, slicing, measuring, stirring.
- **Mission notes:** This is a very rich dish and may suit the palate of older troopers.

TIME NEEDED: 3 HOURS 30 MINUTES • SERVES: 4 • COST: £ £ £ £ £

INGREDIENTS:

- 3 tbsp cooking oil
- Half a leg of lamb (about 1¼ kg)
- 4 large onions, thinly sliced
- Optional: Handful of thyme sprigs
- Seasoning to taste (salt and pepper)
- 300 ml red wine (the alcohol will cook off, don't worry)

INSTRUCTIONS:

1. Preheat oven to 160°C.

2. Heat the oil on the hob in the casserole dish.

3. Brown the meat on all sides, remove and set aside.

4. Place the onions in the casserole dish and fry for 10 minutes, until softened and slightly browned.

5 Add a few of the thyme sprigs if using and cook for a further minute or so.

6 Season if required.

7 Place the lamb on top of the onions, add the wine and the lid.

8 Place in the oven and cook for 3 hours, and then serve.

CHICKEN AND CHORIZO PASTA

Mission brief

- **Kit:** Chopping board and knife, large saucepan, steamer (or saucepan with a lid), large frying pan, and a colander, large saucepan or wok.
- **Skills:** Measuring, stirring, dicing.

TIME NEEDED: 1 HOUR • SERVES: 4 • COST: £ £ £ £ £

INGREDIENTS:

- 350 g pasta
- 350 g broccoli, chopped into small florets
- 2 tbsp cooking oil
- 200 g chorizo sausage, skinned and diced
- 200 g boneless and skinless chicken breast, chopped into chunks
- 90 g basil pesto

INSTRUCTIONS:

1. Boil a large pan of water, cook the pasta according to the packet instructions, drain and set aside.

2. Prepare your steamer and ensure your water is hot and producing steam before adding the broccoli. Steam for 5 minutes and test. Cook no longer than 7 minutes as the vibrant colour will start to be lost. Remove from heat.

3. Heat the oil in a large frying pan and fry the chorizo for 3–4 minutes on a fairly high heat to release juices. Remove the chorizo and set aside.

④ Add the chicken pieces to the frying pan containing the chorizo juices and fry, stirring continuously, at a fairly high heat for 7–10 minutes until cooked through.

⑤ Place the cooked pasta, broccoli, chorizo and chicken in a colander, larger frying pan or wok and stir in the pesto.

⑥ Gently reheat and serve.

CREAMY TOMATO PASTA WITH SAUSAGE

Mission brief

- **Kit:** Chopping board and knife, garlic press (optional), large saucepan.
- **Skills:** Chopping, grating, measuring.
- **Mission notes:** This delicious dish works with vegetarian sausage, or without any sausage at all, if you prefer.

TIME NEEDED: 45 MINUTES • SERVES: 4 • COST: £ £ £ £ £

INGREDIENTS:

- 350 g your favourite pasta
- 1 tbsp cooking oil
- 1 medium onion, finely chopped
- 1 clove garlic, crushed or chopped
- 4 thick pork sausages, skinned
- 1 x 400 g can chopped tomatoes
- 50 g Parmesan, grated
- 2 tbsp double cream or mascarpone

INSTRUCTIONS:

1. Boil a large pan of water, cook the pasta according to the packet instructions, drain and set aside.

2. Heat the oil in the saucepan and fry the onion gently for 3 minutes. Add the garlic and fry for another minute.

3. Crumble the sausage meat into the pan with the onions and garlic, and cook for 6–7 minutes until the sausage meat is lightly browned.

4. Add the can of chopped tomatoes, stir together well, then let the mixture simmer gently for 15 minutes.

5. Add the majority of the Parmesan, cream or mascarpone and stir together well.

6. To serve, add cooked pasta to the pan and stir through, or serve on top, or on the side. The choice is yours!

7. Sprinkle with the remaining Parmesan on top and serve.

SPANISH CHICKEN

Mission brief

- **Kit:** Chopping board and knife, garlic press (optional), can opener.
- **Skills:** Chopping, slicing, peeling, measuring.

TIME NEEDED: 1 HOUR 30 MINUTES • SERVES: 4 •
COST: £ £ £ £ £

INGREDIENTS:

- 1 tbsp cooking oil
- 1 large onion, finely chopped
- 2 red peppers, deseeded and chopped
- 2 garlic cloves, minced or chopped
- 3 tsp smoked paprika
- 4 chicken breasts, cut into strips
- 2 x 400 g cans chopped tomatoes
- 1 tbsp tomato purée
- 1 bay leaf
- Seasoning to taste (salt and pepper)

INSTRUCTIONS:

1. Preheat oven to 180°C.

2. Heat the oil in a large frying pan and fry the onions, peppers and garlic until softened.

3. Add the paprika, stir well and cook for a further minute.

4. Add the chicken strips and fry until they begin to colour (3–4 minutes).

5. Add tinned tomatoes, purée, bay leaf and seasoning to taste (salt and pepper).

6 Bring to the boil, transfer ingredients to an ovenproof dish and cook in the preheated oven for an hour.

7 Remove the bay leaf before serving.

TAKEOUT AT BASE CAMP

Everyone loves a takeout every now and again. By preparing these healthier recipes at base camp you get all the flavour for a fraction of the cost.

What's more, your troopers will love to get involved, especially if you're making one of their favourites.

FISH FINGER WRAPS AND CRUNCHY COLESLAW

SERVE WITH: Cherry tomatoes and diced cucumber.

Mission brief

- **Kit:** Two shallow bowls, large plate, baking tray, grater, large bowl, chopping board and knife, spatula, measuring scales and tablespoon.
- **Skills:** Greasing, beating, shredding, breading, measuring.

TIME NEEDED: 1 HOUR 10 MINUTES • SERVES: 4 •
COST: £ £ £ £ £

INGREDIENTS:

For the coleslaw:
- 1 carrot, grated
- ½ red pepper, finely shredded
- ½ celery stalk, finely shredded
- 1 spring onion, finely shredded

For the fish fingers:
- 1 tsp cooking oil
- 1 egg, beaten
- 50 g breadcrumbs
- 300 g skinless filleted white fish (haddock, whiting, cod, pollock, etc.), fresh or defrosted, cut into fingers

For the wraps:
- 4 medium-sized wraps
- A little ketchup or mayonnaise

INSTRUCTIONS:

1. Prepare the coleslaw ingredients, place in a bowl, cover and put in the fridge.

2. Preheat the oven to 200°C.

3. Grease the baking tray with the cooking oil.

4. In the first shallow bowl:
   - Break the egg and lightly beat until thoroughly mixed.

5. In the second shallow bowl:
   - Place the breadcrumbs.

6. Take each fish finger and dip it into the egg until fully coated, then into the breadcrumbs until fully covered. Then place on the plate.

7. When all fish fingers are complete, place on the baking tray and put in the oven for 15 minutes, turning the tray halfway through.

8. Lay out the wraps and spread a little ketchup or mayonnaise on each to help stick it together (this isn't essential – my daughter doesn't like any sauces and it still works).

9. Pile the coleslaw in the centre of each wrap, vertically.

10. When the fish is ready, remove from the oven and put on top of the coleslaw.

11. Wrap as described on the facing page, cut in half and serve.

TIP: You can put whatever you like into your coleslaw, just shred it finely and include "juicy" vegetables like celery and carrot to keep it all together. Red cabbage and leeks work well because they have such great textures.

WRAP LIKE A PRO

1 Fold the sides of the wrap halfway toward the centre.

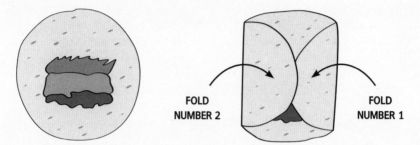

2 Fold the bottom third up toward the centre.

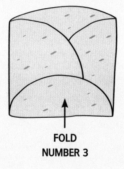

3 Start to wrap, continually tucking your filling back in as you roll it up, until you reach the end.

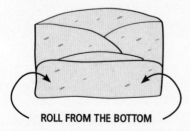

"WRAPPED LIKE A PRO!"

BURGERS

I am a huge fan of home-made burgers. Here I include instructions for veggie burgers, turkey burgers and the classic beef burgers. Serve in your favourite kind of bun with lettuce and tomato – and at the end of the chapter have a look at the recipes for home-made sauces.

VEGGIE BURGERS

Mission brief

- **Kit:** Frying pan, clean knife and chopping board, clean tea towel for draining the courgettes, mixing bowl, garlic press (optional), grater, spatula.
- **Skills:** Chopping, grating, binding, frying.

TIME NEEDED: 1 HOUR • MAKES: 4 BURGERS • COST: £ £ £ £ £

INGREDIENTS:

- 2 medium courgettes, grated
- 2 medium carrots, grated
- 3 tbsp cooking oil (1 tbsp for frying, 2 tbsp for binding)
- 1 large onion, chopped
- 1 clove of garlic, minced or chopped
- 1 tsp ground cumin
- 1 tsp ground coriander
- 2 tbsp chopped fresh coriander
- Seasoning to taste (salt and pepper)
- 1 egg
- 100 g breadcrumbs

INSTRUCTIONS:

1. Wrap the prepared courgettes in a clean tea towel and squeeze them over the sink to remove as much fluid as possible. Place them in the bowl with the prepared carrot.

2. Heat ½ tbsp of the oil in a large frying pan and gently fry the onion and garlic for 5 minutes, stirring frequently, until the onion is soft and beginning to brown.

3. Add the carrots and courgettes, and fry for a further 10 minutes, stirring, until the vegetables have softened.

4. Stir in the ground cumin and coriander, fresh coriander and seasoning to taste, and mix well.

5. Remove the pan from the heat and set aside to cool.

6. Beat the egg in a large bowl and mix all the vegetables, 2 tbsp oil and breadcrumbs until ingredients are thoroughly combined.

7. Using your hands, divide ingredients into four burgers.

8. Heat the remaining ½ tbsp oil in the frying pan and gently fry the burgers for about 5 minutes on each side, or until they are firm and golden, then serve.

TURKEY BURGERS

Mission brief

- **Kit:** Chopping board and knife, frying pan, mixing bowl, measuring scales and spoons, kitchen roll on a plate.
- **Skills:** Measuring, chopping, mixing, frying, binding.

TIME NEEDED: 45 MINUTES • MAKES: 4 BURGERS • COST: £ £ £ £ £

INGREDIENTS:

- 6 tbsp cooking oil (3 tbsp for binding, 3 tbsp for frying)
- 1 small onion, finely diced
- 450 g minced turkey
- Seasoning to taste (salt and pepper)
- Optional: If you'd like to spice up your burgers, use 1 tsp smoked paprika

INSTRUCTIONS:

1. Heat 1 tbsp oil in a large frying pan and gently fry the onion until golden.
2. Put the onions into the mixing bowl and allow to cool slightly.
3. Add turkey mince and seasoning to taste (salt and pepper).
4. Combine ingredients with 3 tbsp of oil until well mixed.
5. Using your hands, divide ingredients into four burgers.
6. Heat the remaining oil in the frying pan.
7. Fry each burger for approximately 15–20 minutes, turning regularly to avoid burning, until juices from the burgers run clear.
8. Place the burgers on the kitchen roll to remove any surplus oil then serve.

BEEF BURGERS

Mission brief

- **Kit:** Garlic press (optional), chopping board and knife, frying pan, mixing bowl, measuring scales and spoons, kitchen roll on a plate.
- **Skills:** Chopping, mixing, frying, binding, measuring.

TIME NEEDED: 45 MINUTES • MAKES: 4 BURGERS • COST: £ £ £ £ £

INGREDIENTS:

- 1 tbsp cooking oil
- 1 small onion, finely chopped
- 1 garlic clove, minced or chopped
- 500 g lean minced beef
- 50 g breadcrumbs, you can make these if you have slightly stale bread and a hand blender
- 1 egg
- Seasoning to taste (salt and pepper)

INSTRUCTIONS:

1. Heat the oil in a frying pan and gently fry the onion and garlic for 3 minutes.
2. Put into a mixing bowl and leave to cool slightly.
3. Place all remaining ingredients in the bowl and mix together well.
4. Using your hands, divide ingredients into four burgers.
5. Cook under a medium grill for about 4–5 minutes on each side.
6. Place the burgers on the kitchen roll to remove any surplus oil then serve.

FRENCH BREAD PIZZA

Mission brief

- **Kit:** Garlic press (optional), chopping board and knife, bread knife, grater, baking sheet, pastry brush, medium saucepan, can opener.
- **Skills:** Grating, brushing, cutting.
- **Mission notes:** This recipe is a classic cheese and tomato pizza, but don't be afraid to experiment with toppings.

TIME NEEDED: 1 HOUR • SERVES: 4 • COST: £ £ £ £ £

INGREDIENTS:

- 4 tbsp olive oil
- 3 tbsp butter
- 4 garlic cloves, minced or chopped
- ½ tsp dried oregano or mixed herbs
- 1 large stick of French bread
- 1 x 400 g tin chopped tomatoes
- 100 g mozzarella, grated

INSTRUCTIONS:

1. Preheat the oven to 210°C.

2. Grease a baking tray with a little of the oil (¼ tsp).

3. Heat butter and the rest of the olive oil in a medium saucepan over low–medium heat until butter is melted.

4. Add garlic and oregano and cook for 2 minutes, until garlic is softened.

5. Slice the French stick in half horizontally and squash both halves down to keep them stable on the tray.

6. Brush half of the garlic and oregano mixture on top of the bread.

7. Add the chopped tomatoes to the remaining garlic mixture in the pan and bring to a simmer. Simmer for 15 minutes to thicken, stirring occasionally. Leave to cool slightly.

8. Spread tomato sauce evenly over bread, and add mozzarella on top of sauce.

9. Place in an oven and bake until cheese is melted and just starting to brown, about 10–15 minutes, and serve.

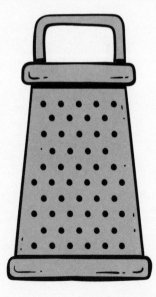

CHINESE CHICKEN

SERVE WITH: Egg fried rice (see page 142).

Mission brief
- **Kit:** Grater, garlic press (optional), chopping board and knife, ovenproof dish, measuring spoons.
- **Skills:** Grating, measuring, taking the temperature of meat.
- **Mission notes:** This dish is best started a couple of hours ahead so the marinade can thoroughly sink into the meat – leave it overnight in the fridge if you can.

**TIME NEEDED: 1 HOUR 30 MINUTES • SERVES: 4 •
COST: £ £ £ £ £**

INGREDIENTS:

- 3-cm piece of fresh ginger, peeled and grated
- 1 garlic clove, minced or chopped finely
- 2 tbsp clear honey
- 2 tsp Chinese five spice

- 2 tsp soy sauce
- 1 tbsp sesame oil
- 4 chicken drumsticks
- 4 chicken wings

INSTRUCTIONS:

To prepare the chicken in the marinade:

1. Prepare the ginger, garlic and mix with the honey, spices, soy sauce and oil. This is the marinade.

2 Place the chicken in the dish, coat with the marinade, cover and put in the fridge for at least half an hour, but overnight if possible.

To cook:

1 Preheat oven to 180°C.

2 Take the dish with the chicken out of the fridge.

3 Place the dish into the preheated oven and cook for about 30 minutes, turning occasionally and basting with the marinade and juices until thoroughly sticky and golden.

4 Check the chicken is cooked through by either using your meat thermometer (should read min. 75°C), or seeing if the juices run clear when the meat is pierced, then serve.

BEEF BURRITO

Mission brief

- **Kit:** Garlic press (optional), chopping board and sharp knife, measuring scales and spoons, small saucepan, colander, large saucepan, frying pan.
- **Skills:** Measuring, chopping, grating, frying, making wraps.

TIME NEEDED: 1 HOUR AND 15 MINUTES • SERVES: 6 • COST: £ £ £ £ £

INGREDIENTS:

- 240 g cooked brown rice or 80 g uncooked
- 2 tbsp cooking oil
- 1 medium onion, finely chopped
- 2 garlic cloves, minced or finely chopped
- 500 g beef mince
- ½ tbsp ground cumin
- ½ tbsp paprika
- ¼ tsp chilli powder (mild, or go hotter if your troopers like it)
- 2 tsp tomato purée
- 400 g tin chopped tomatoes
- 210 g tin black beans, drained
- 75 ml beef stock
- 4 tbsp chopped coriander
- Seasoning to taste (salt and pepper)
- 8 medium wraps
- 100 g Cheddar cheese, grated

INSTRUCTIONS:

1. If you have no pre-prepared cooked rice, bring a small saucepan of water to the boil and make the rice according to packet instructions. Drain, rinse and leave in a colander.

2 Heat half the oil in the large saucepan over a medium–high heat, add the onion and garlic and sauté for 5–6 minutes, stirring occasionally, until the onion starts to brown.

3 Crumble the beef mince into the saucepan and turn the heat up.

4 Cook for 3 minutes, stirring continuously to break up meat, until browned all over.

5 Stir in the cumin, paprika, chilli powder and tomato purée, and cook for 1 minute.

6 Add the chopped tomatoes, black beans and stock to the pan. Stir and bring to the boil.

7 Reduce the heat to a simmer and cook for 20 minutes until thickened, stirring occasionally.

8 Remove from the heat, stir in the chopped coriander, season to taste and let cool slightly.

9 In the centre of each wrap, add rice, mince mixture and cheese.

10 See Wrap Like a Pro on page 118 for how to wrap each burrito.

11 Heat a little of the remaining oil in a frying pan and, taking a few of the burritos at a time, brown on all sides, pressing them down into the pan to help the outside get crispy, and serve.

CRUNCHY CHICKEN NUGGETS

Mission brief

- **Kit:** Sieve, non-stick baking parchment or greaseproof paper, two shallow bowls, baking tray, two large plates, plastic bag, rolling pin.
- **Skills:** Beating, cutting, sifting, dipping and coating.

TIME NEEDED: 45 MINUTES • SERVES: 4 • COST: £ £ £ £ £

INGREDIENTS:

- Butter or oil for greasing
- 3 tbsp plain flour
- 1 tsp smoked paprika
- 1 egg
- Splash of soy sauce (or water if you don't like soy sauce)
- 125 g cornflakes
- 500 g skinless chicken breasts, cut into nugget size

INSTRUCTIONS:

1. Preheat the oven to 200°C.

2. Grease a baking tray and line with baking paper.

3. Sift the flour and paprika onto a large plate.

4. In the first shallow bowl:
   - Beat the egg and add a splash of soy sauce.

5. In the second shallow bowl:
   - Add the cornflakes to the plastic bag and gently crush them with the rolling pin. Place in the bowl.

⑥ Take each piece of chicken:

- Dip the chicken into the flour, ensuring it is covered and shake off the excess.
- Dip the chicken into the egg.
- Dip the chicken into the cornflakes.
- Place on the plate.

⑦ When all the chicken nuggets are complete, place on the baking tray and put in the oven for 15–20 minutes. Check that they are cooked through, place on the second large plate and serve.

CHICKEN FAJITAS

Mission brief

- **Kit:** Wok or large saucepan, measuring scales and spoons, garlic press (optional), chopping board and sharp knife, juicer, plate.
- **Skills:** Cutting, juicing, mixing, frying, grating, wrapping.
- **Mission notes:** This dish is best started a couple of hours ahead so the marinade can thoroughly sink into the meat – leave it overnight in the fridge if you can.

TIME NEEDED: 1 HOUR 30 MINUTES • SERVES: 4 •
COST: £ £ £ £ £

INGREDIENTS:

For the marinade:

- 4 tbsp olive oil
- 1 tsp lime juice
- 1 tsp mild chilli powder
- 1 tsp paprika
- 1 tsp caster sugar
- ½ tsp ground cumin
- 1 garlic clove, minced or chopped
- 1 tsp salt

For the fajitas:

- 400 g chicken breast, fresh or defrosted, cut into strips
- 2 red peppers, deseeded and sliced
- 1 medium red onion, finely sliced
- 2 tbsp vegetable oil
- 8 medium wraps
- 100 ml sour cream or plain yoghurt
- 100 g Cheddar cheese, grated

INSTRUCTIONS:

1. Mix the marinade ingredients together in a bowl.

2. Prepare the chicken and add to the marinade. Cover and put in the fridge for at least an hour but overnight if possible.

3. When ready to make the fajitas, prepare the pepper and onion.

4. Heat the oil in the wok over a high heat and stir-fry the chicken, pepper and onion for 6–8 minutes, or until the chicken is cooked through.

5. Lay your wraps on a plate and warm for a few seconds in the microwave.

6. In the centre of each wrap, place the fajita mixture, cream and cheese.

7. Fold over one side of the wrap into the middle of the fajita, and then the other side into the centre.

8. Serve and enjoy!

SAUCES AND SIDES

We all have cupboards full of half eaten bottles of sauce. Yet sauces take minutes to make, taste delicious home-made and, of course, if we're making them ourselves, we know exactly what goes into them.

It's the same with sides – they're straightforward to make at a fraction of the cost of buying them. You'll find garlic bread and egg fried rice in this section, but in The Trimmings (page 143) you'll also find Yorkshire puddings, roast potatoes and cauliflower cheese.

You can't do without the trimmings. They add to a meal and turn it into a celebration.

GUACAMOLE

Mission brief

- **Kit:** Chopping board and knife, garlic press (optional), juicer, fork for mashing, medium bowl.
- **Skills:** Chopping, juicing, mashing.

TIME NEEDED: 30 MINUTES • SERVES: 4 • COST: £ £ £ £ £

INGREDIENTS:

- 2 ripe avocados, stoned and chopped
- 1 small red onion, finely chopped
- 1 clove garlic, minced or finely chopped
- 1 ripe tomato, finely chopped
- 1 lime, juiced
- Seasoning to taste (salt and pepper)

INSTRUCTIONS:

1. Mash avocados in a medium serving bowl and stir in onion, garlic, tomato and lime juice.

2. Season with salt and pepper to taste and serve.

BARBECUE SAUCE

Mission brief

- **Kit:** Jar to serve (and store any spare in the fridge), small whisk, medium-sized mixing bowl, measuring scales and spoons.
- **Skills:** Whisking, measuring.

TIME NEEDED: 10 MINUTES • SERVES: 4–8 • COST: £ £ £ £ £

INGREDIENTS:

- 170 g ketchup
- 1 tbsp white wine vinegar
- 2 tsp smoked paprika
- 2 tbsp light brown sugar
- 1 tbsp Worcestershire sauce

INSTRUCTIONS:

1. Whisk all ingredients together in a medium-sized bowl.

2. Spoon into glass jar and store in fridge until needed, then serve.

3. Any leftovers will keep in the fridge for five days.

BURGER SAUCE

Mission brief

- **Kit:** Glass jar to serve (and store any spare in the fridge), small whisk, small mixing bowl, chopping board and knife.
- **Skills:** Whisking, chopping.

TIME NEEDED: 15 MINUTES • SERVES: 4–6 • COST: £ £ £ £ £

INGREDIENTS:

- 4 tbsp mayonnaise
- 2 tsp yellow mustard
- 2 tsp tomato ketchup
- 1 gherkin, finely chopped

INSTRUCTIONS:

1. Whisk the mayonnaise, yellow mustard and tomato ketchup together in a small bowl.

2. Add the gherkin to the mixture.

3. Spoon into glass jar and store in fridge until needed, then serve.

4. Any leftovers will keep in the fridge for five days.

MARIE ROSE SAUCE

Mission brief

- **Kit:** Glass jar to serve (and store any spare in the fridge), small whisk, small mixing bowl, measuring spoons, juicer.
- **Skills:** Whisking, juicing.
- **Mission notes:** This sauce is great with prawns – it's your classic prawn cocktail sauce but works great in prawn sandwiches too.

TIME NEEDED: 10 MINUTES • SERVES: 2 • COST: £ £ £ £ £

INGREDIENTS:

- 3 heaped tbsp mayonnaise
- 2 heaped tbsp tomato ketchup
- Squeeze of lemon
- Pinch of salt
- Optional: pinch of smoked paprika

INSTRUCTIONS:

1. Whisk everything together in a small bowl.

2. If possible, chill in the fridge for a couple of hours before using, then serve.

3. Spoon any unused sauce into a clean jar and keep in the fridge for three days.

CUCUMBER MINT RAITA

Mission brief

- **Kit:** Mixing bowl, clean tea towel, chopping board and knife, peeler.
- **Skills:** Chopping, peeling, mixing.

TIME NEEDED: 10 MINUTES • SERVES: 4–8 • COST: £ £ £ £ £

INGREDIENTS:

- ½ cucumber, peeled and chopped
- 150 g natural yoghurt
- 1 tsp mint sauce or 1 tbsp finely chopped mint leaves
- Pinch of salt
- Pinch of sugar, to taste

INSTRUCTIONS:

1. Wrap the prepared cucumber in a clean tea towel and squeeze over the sink to remove as much fluid as possible.

2. Mix the cucumber in a bowl with all the other ingredients.

3. Cover and keep in the fridge until ready to serve.

4. Any leftovers will keep in the fridge for three days.

HOME-MADE GRAVY

Mission brief

- **Kit:** Large frying pan, scales, chopping board and knife, wooden spoon.
- **Skills:** Measuring, stirring, frying, cutting, caramelizing.

INGREDIENTS:

- 15 g butter
- 1 onion, thinly sliced
- 1 tsp sugar
- 1 tbsp plain flour
- 2 beef stock cubes (for 400 ml of stock)

INSTRUCTIONS:

1. Melt the butter in a frying pan.

2. Add the onion and sprinkle with sugar.

3. Fry the onions gently, stirring occasionally, for 10–15 minutes or until they are soft and lightly caramelized.

4. Sprinkle the flour over the onion, stir and cook for 1 minute.

5. Gradually stir in the stock.

6. Bring to the boil, then reduce the heat and leave to simmer gently until thickened and serve.

GARLIC BREAD

Mission brief

- **Kit:** Bread knife and chopping board, garlic press (optional), sharp knife, small mixing bowl, kitchen foil.
- **Skills:** Cutting, buttering, mixing.

TIME NEEDED: 35 MINUTES • SERVES: 4–6 • COST: £ £ £ £ £

INGREDIENTS:

- 2 cloves garlic, minced or chopped finely
- 150 g butter, softened
- 1 tsp dried parsley
- 1 stick French bread

INSTRUCTIONS:

1. Preheat the oven to 190°C.

2. Mix the prepared garlic in a small bowl with the butter and parsley.

3. Prepare the French stick by cutting about three quarters through at 4-cm intervals along the stick.

4. Spread the garlic butter on both sides of every cut along the loaf.

5. Wrap the loaf in foil, making sure all gaps are closed.

6. Place in the oven and cook for 15–20 minutes, then serve.

EGG FRIED RICE

Mission brief

- **Kit:** Measuring scales and spoons, large saucepan, large frying pan or wok, colander.
- **Skills:** Measuring, rinsing, frying, beating.

TIME NEEDED: 45 MINUTES • SERVES: 4 • COST: £ £ £ £ £

INGREDIENTS:

- 300 g long grain rice
- 2 eggs
- 2 tbsp cooking oil
- 100 g frozen peas
- 100 g frozen or canned sweetcorn
- Soy sauce, to season
- Black pepper, to season

INSTRUCTIONS:

1. Bring water to boil in a large saucepan, and cook the rice according to the packet instructions.

2. Drain, rinse well with cold water and leave for 15–20 minutes to drain thoroughly in a colander.

3. Beat the eggs and set aside.

4. Heat the oil in the large frying pan or wok and add the cold cooked rice, peas and sweetcorn. Stir-fry over a medium–high heat for 2–3 minutes.

5. Add the egg and stir everything together until the eggs have set.

6. Season with soy sauce and black pepper, and serve.

THE TRIMMINGS

Mission brief

- **Mission notes**: For all the trimmings, I have recommended an oven temperature. However, if you're roasting meat in the oven, you will need to cook at that temperature and adjust your heating times accordingly.

YORKSHIRE PUDDINGS

Mission brief

- **Kit**: 12-hole muffin tray, bowl, whisk.
- **Skills**: Mixing, whisking.
- **Mission notes**: You'll need to leave this batter for at least half an hour before cooking (and it can be left for up to 12 hours)

TIME NEEDED: 1 HOUR 15 MINUTES • SERVES: 6 (2 EACH) • COST: £ £ £ £ £

INGREDIENTS:

- 3 eggs
- 115 g plain flour
- 275 ml milk
- 2–3 tbsp vegetable oil

INSTRUCTIONS:

1. Preheat the oven to 240°C.

2. Mix together the eggs and flour.

3. Add the milk, gently whisking until you have a runny batter.

4. Cover and leave this to rest in the fridge for any length of time between half an hour and 12 hours.

5. When ready to cook, drizzle a little oil in the bottom of each of the compartments of the muffin tray.

6. Heat the oil in the oven for about 10 minutes, until it is piping hot.

7. Remove the tin from the oven, pour in the batter, and immediately return to the oven.

8. Bake for 25 minutes, until golden brown and crispy and serve.

⚠️ **WARNING:**

Do not open the oven door for the first 20 minutes – your yorkies will sink.

CAULIFLOWER CHEESE

Mission brief

- **Kit:** Saucepan, colander, measuring jug and spoons, whisk – a silicone handle will reduce the chance of burns, ovenproof dish, oven gloves, grater.
- **Skills:** Measuring, whisking a sauce (hot).

TIME NEEDED: 1 HOUR • SERVES: 6 • COST: £ £ £ £ £

INGREDIENTS:

- 1 head of cauliflower, broken into florets
- Cheese sauce (see page 54)

INSTRUCTIONS:

1. Preheat the oven to 210°C (unless you're already cooking a joint and then put it in at that temperature and monitor it).

2. Prepare the cauliflower and boil or steam it until it is soft but with some bite left in it (al dente).

3. While your cauliflower is cooking, prepare a cheese sauce, using the recipe on page 54.

4. Tip your cauliflower into an ovenproof dish and cover with the cheese sauce.

5. Bake in the oven for 20 minutes until the cheese sauce is bubbling and serve.

ROAST POTATOES

Mission brief

- **Kit:** Large saucepan with lid, roasting tin, potato peeler, chopping board and knife, colander, oven gloves.
- **Skills:** Peeling, chopping.
- **Mission notes:** I love a roast potato with a crunchy outside, so the trick is to rough up the outside of the potatoes and then add a sprinkling of flour before roasting in a hot oven.

TIME NEEDED: 1 HOUR 15 MINUTES • SERVES: 4–6 •
COST: £ £ £ £ £

INGREDIENTS:

- 1 kg floury potatoes, such as Maris Piper, peeled and cut to equal sized roasties
- Salt
- 100 ml olive oil, vegetable oil or goose fat
- 1 tbsp plain flour

INSTRUCTIONS:

1. Preheat oven to 200°C.

2. Place the potatoes in a pan of cold, salted water with a lid to bring to the boil.

3. Add the oil to the roasting pan and put it in the oven to heat until the oil smokes – at least 20 minutes.

4. Boil potatoes for 5 minutes, drain in a colander and return to the saucepan.

5 Sprinkle a tbsp of flour over the potatoes, put the lid back on and hold it as you shake the pan as hard as you can. The spuds should look well and truly rough around the edges.

6 Check the oil and if it's smoking hot, bring it out. If not, wait a few minutes.

7 When ready, take the roasting tin out of the oven and add the potatoes.

8 Make sure the potatoes are fully coated in the hot fat.

9 Return to the oven for 50 minutes to an hour – until the potatoes are golden and crunchy on the outside and soft in the middle. Turn them over once during cooking and serve when cooked.

BREAKFASTS

All the recipes in this section are nutritious – but also quick to make, as breakfast can be one of the busiest times at base camp. In the case of overnight French Toast, you can prep the night before and pop into the oven before you do reveille – and then the troops can wake up to the smell of warm cinnamon. Delicious.

PORRIDGE

Mission brief
- **Kit:** Saucepan, measuring scales and jug.
- **Skills:** Measuring, stirring.

TIME NEEDED: 20 MINUTES • SERVES: 2 • COST: £££££

INGREDIENTS:
- 100 g porridge oats
- 100 ml milk
- 300 ml boiling water
- Toppings (see below)

INSTRUCTIONS:
1. Put oats and milk into the saucepan and mix to a paste.
2. Add boiling water.
3. Bring to a boil and then reduce to a simmer.
4. Simmer for 15 minutes, stirring occasionally.
5. Pour into two bowls and allow to cool.
6. Add toppings and serve.

TOPPINGS:
- Sliced banana
- Berries (fresh or defrosted)
- 1 tbsp nuts or seeds
- Swirl of honey or maple syrup
- 1 tbsp of jam

BREAKFAST SMOOTHIE

Mission brief

- **Kit:** Blender.
- **Skills:** Measuring, peeling bananas, blending – noisy but popular.
- **Mission notes:** Smoothies are quick, healthy and a great way to use ripe and overripe fruit. Try to use fruit in season – it's better for the environment and your wallet. Frozen fruit is great too, and you won't need to use so much ice. Below are some great recipes to get you started.

TIME NEEDED: 5 MINUTES • SERVES: 1 • COST: £ £ £ £ £

INGREDIENTS:

- 1 large banana
- 200 ml milk (or milk alternative – coconut milk is nice)
- 2 tbsp rolled porridge oats
- 2 tsp runny honey
- 2 ice cubes

INSTRUCTIONS:

1. Add all the ingredients to your blender.

2. Blend until smooth.

3. Serve immediately.

VARIATIONS (ALL SERVE 1):

Banana and raspberry smoothie:
INGREDIENTS:

- 1 large banana
- 120 ml milk (or milk alternative)
- 60 ml natural yoghurt
- 90 g raspberries
- 2 ice cubes

Strawberry smoothie:
INGREDIENTS:

- ¼ cantaloupe melon, peeled and cubed, with seeds removed
- 5 strawberries, washed with leaves removed
- 120 ml milk (or milk alternative)
- 2 ice cubes

SMOOTHIE SURGERY

The great thing about smoothies is that you can taste and adjust them as you go. Here are some trouble-shooting tips to help you make perfect smoothies:

- **Too runny?** Try using less liquid or not blending for so long. As these smoothies contain ice, they need to be eaten soon after they have been made to prevent the ice melting.
- **Too frothy?** I prefer milk, or a milk alternative, in smoothies. However, it can make it frothy. If you don't want a frothy smoothie, use fresh fruit juice instead.
- **Not sweet enough?** Add your preferred sweetener, such as honey or maple syrup.
- **Not blending well?** Are you overfilling the blender? Do you have an older blender that could do with a little help? If so, chop the ingredients smaller and blend before you add the ice. Also try adding a little more liquid.

FRUIT SALAD AND CHEESE

SERVE WITH: Crackers or toasted pitta bread cut into fingers go well with this breakfast.

Mission brief

- **Kit:** Knife and chopping board, bowl.
- **Skills:** Cutting, peeling.
- **Mission notes:** This is a great breakfast for using fresh, ripe fruit that's in season – and the cheese adds protein. I cut the portions small so that they can be eaten with fingers, making it even more fun.

TIME NEEDED: 5 MINUTES • SERVES: 1 • COST: £ £ £ £ £

INGREDIENTS:

- A small plate of fruit, which could include:
  - Grapes, halved
  - Bananas, chopped
  - Berries
  - Melon, peeled and cubed
  - Orange segments
  - Apple (but cut it last as it will brown when it's exposed to the air)
- Cheese, sliced

INSTRUCTIONS:

1. Prepare the fruit and cheese.
2. Assemble on a plate and serve.

TIP: Use your trooper's favourite cheese, but it's also a good opportunity to introduce them to new flavours. I've served this with all kinds of Cheddar cheese, Red Leicester (the colour is a great novelty), mozzarella, feta, Edam, vegan cheese and even cheese triangles.

FRIED EGGS

SERVE WITH: Hot, buttered toast.

Mission brief

- **Kit:** Frying pan, spatula.
- **Skills:** Cracking eggs, frying.
- **Mission brief:** My favourite cooked breakfast item is an egg – they are so quick, versatile, tasty, and have a lot to offer on the nutrition front. Try to buy the eggs fresh as you will get better results when you cook them, and they'll taste better.

TIME NEEDED: 5 MINUTES • SERVES: 1 • COST: £ £ £ £ £

INGREDIENTS:

- 1 or 2 eggs, depending on appetite
- 2 tbsp cooking oil

INSTRUCTIONS:

1. Gently heat oil in a frying pan, but don't let the fat get too hot or the egg will stick to the pan and bubble.

2. Carefully crack the egg on the side of the pan.

3. Fry gently for about 3 minutes, basting occasionally and lifting the edges with a spatula as it cooks to prevent sticking.

4. If you want to cook both sides of the egg, gently turn it, count to ten slowly, and serve.

POACHED EGGS

Mission brief

- **Kit:** Saucepan with lid, slotted spoon, cup or ramekin for breaking eggs into, kitchen towel on a clean plate.
- **Skills:** Cracking eggs, stirring, poaching.

TIME NEEDED: 10 MINUTES • SERVES: 1 • COST: £ £ £ £ £

INGREDIENTS:

- 1 or 2 eggs, depending on appetite – but eggs must be cooked one at a time
- A drop of malt or white wine vinegar

INSTRUCTIONS:

1. Heat water in a lidded pan (at least 5 cm deep) until boiling.

2. Remove the lid from the pan and reduce to a simmer.

3. Break a single egg into a cup or ramekin.

4. Put a drop of vinegar in the water and stir it until you have created a little whirlpool.

5. Slide the egg gently into the centre of the water whirlpool.

6. When the egg has firmed up and the white has become opaque, about 3–4 minutes, remove it carefully with a slotted spoon and put it onto a plate covered with kitchen towel to soak up the excess water, and serve.

SCRAMBLED EGGS

Mission brief
- **Kit:** Mixing bowl, saucepan, whisk, wooden or silicone spoon.
- **Skills:** Cracking eggs, whisking, measuring.

TIME NEEDED: 10 MINUTES • SERVES: 2 • COST: £ £ £ £ £

INGREDIENTS:

- 3 eggs
- 4 tbsp milk
- 25 g butter
- Seasoning to taste (salt and pepper)

INSTRUCTIONS:

1. Break the eggs in a bowl and whisk.

2. Add the milk.

3. Melt the butter in a saucepan before adding the egg mixture (don't let it brown as it will colour your eggs).

4. Stir the mixture gently and slowly but continuously as it thickens.

5. Don't have the heat up too high, or the eggs will burn and stick to the pan.

6. The eggs are done when they have reached your desired consistency – anything from velvety to "crumbly" – the main thing is to tip them out of the pan when ready or they will continue to cook.

7. Serve.

TIP: To remove stray pieces of eggshell from cracked egg, use half of the cracked eggshell. It will attract the stray piece like a magnet and the shape will make it easy for you to scoop it out.

BOILED EGGS

Mission brief

- **Kit:** Saucepan with a lid, bowl of cold water (not needed if making runny egg and soldiers), slotted spoon, egg cups for runny and soft eggs, knife and chopping board for hard-boiled eggs.
- **Skills:** Peeling eggs.

**TIME NEEDED: UP TO 20 MINUTES • SERVES: 1 •
COST: £££££**

INGREDIENTS:

- 1 or 2 eggs per person, depending on appetite

INSTRUCTIONS:

1. Heat water in a lidded pan to a rolling boil.

2. Fill a bowl with cold water if making soft- or hard-boiled eggs.

3. Remove the lid.

4. Add eggs carefully using a slotted spoon.

5. Time your eggs as follows:

   - 5 minutes: A runny egg. Take the egg out of the water with a slotted spoon and put it into your egg cup. Take the top off straight away or the egg will continue to cook.

   - 7 minutes: A soft-boiled egg. Repeat the steps for a runny egg (above).

- 10 minutes: A hard-boiled egg. Remove the egg from the water with a slotted spoon and place in a bowl of cold water. When ready to eat, peel and eat (perfect for picnics). If using in a recipe, cut on a chopping board.

HOW TO PEEL AN EGG

1. Put the cooked egg in a bowl of cold water as this loosens the membrane between the egg white and shell.

2. Leave for one minute.

3. Drain the water and gently crack the egg shell.

4. Add more cold water.

5. After a minute or two, gently tap the eggs on the clean counter or chopping board to break the shell all over before peeling.

PANCAKES

Mission brief

- **Kit:** Measuring scales, spoons and jug, bowl, spatula, jug, whisk, frying pan.
- **Skills:** Stirring, beating, measuring, frying, flipping.

TIME NEEDED: 10 MINUTES • SERVES: 4 • COST: £ £ £ £ £

INGREDIENTS:

- 100 g plain flour
- 1 egg
- 250 ml milk
- 2 tbsp cooking oil
- Toppings (see facing page)

INSTRUCTIONS:

1. Put the flour in a bowl and add the egg into the middle.

2. Pour in about a third of the milk.

3. Stir gently, adding the rest of the milk a little at a time.

4. Beat the mixture thoroughly, then pour into a jug.

5. Heat a few drops of oil in the frying pan until it's nice and hot, then add a couple of tablespoons of the batter.

6. Tip the frying pan to spread the mixture evenly – the aim is to create as thin a layer as possible.

7. Fry until the underside is brown, using a spatula to lift the edges so that they don't stick, then toss the pancake (or, if there's no one around to impress, you could flip the pancake using a spatula or palette knife).

8 Tip finished pancakes onto a plate and continue cooking pancakes until you have used all your batter (or have made as many pancakes as will be eaten), add toppings and serve.

TOPPINGS:

- Lemon juice and sugar
- Sliced strawberries and chocolate spread
- Chopped banana and a swirl of honey
- Chopped banana and peanut butter
- Berries and yoghurt

OVERNIGHT FRENCH TOAST

SERVE WITH: You can serve French toast on its own, but if you want something to accompany it, try toppings such as fresh fruit, a little sieved icing sugar or maple syrup, sausage or bacon.

Mission brief

- **Kit:** Bowl, whisk, ovenproof dish, chopping board and bread knife, measuring spoons and jug, cling film (or something to cover the ovenproof dish to avoid single-use plastic, such as a clean plastic tray).
- **Skills:** Beating, cutting, measuring.
- **Mission notes:** The beauty of this recipe is that it can be easily prepared the night before and put in the oven in the morning for a fuss-free cooked breakfast, and the smell of warm French toast will help even the most tired sleepyheads get out of bed!

**TIME NEEDED: PREP: 15 MINUTES;
BAKING: 25–30 MINUTES • SERVES: 4 • COST: £££££**

INGREDIENTS:

- 3 eggs
- 200 ml milk
- ¼ tsp baking powder
- ¼ tsp cinnamon
- 1 tsp vanilla essence
- 2 tbsp sugar
- 6 slices bread

INSTRUCTIONS:

To prepare:

1. In a bowl, beat the eggs, milk, baking powder, cinnamon, vanilla essence and sugar until well combined.

2. Cut each slice of bread into four pieces and place in the ovenproof dish.

3. Pour the batter over the bread or, if you prefer, dip the bread in the mixture before arranging in the dish.

4. Cover the French toast before refrigerating overnight.

To cook:

1. Take the French toast out of the fridge.

2. Preheat the oven to 180°C.

3. Bake for 25–30 minutes and serve.

EGGY BREAD

Mission brief
- **Kit:** Bowl, whisk, frying pan, chopping board and knife, spatula.
- **Skills:** Beating, measuring, frying.

**TIME NEEDED: PREP: 10 MINUTES;
BAKING: 10 MINUTES • SERVES: 2 • COST: £ £ £ £ £**

INGREDIENTS:

- 2 eggs
- 1 tbsp milk
- Seasoning to taste (salt and pepper)
- 2 slices of bread
- 1 tbsp cooking oil

INSTRUCTIONS:

1. Break the eggs into a bowl and beat them lightly.

2. Stir in the milk and add seasoning to taste (salt and pepper) if required.

3. Slice the bread into halves.

4. Heat the oil in a frying pan.

5. Dip the bread into the egg, then place the bread into the frying pan and fry until both sides are golden brown.

6. Remove from the pan and serve immediately.

PACKED LUNCHES AND PICNICS

There's minimal cooking required in this section, but rest assured, there's still maximum taste. Variety is the spice of life and if your trooper takes a packed lunch, you can use the ideas here to keep things interesting.

SAUSAGE ROLLS

Mission brief

- **Kit:** Small bowl, chopping board and knife, baking tray, pastry brush, spatula.
- **Skills:** Cutting pastry, glazing.

TIME NEEDED: 50 MINUTES •
MAKES: 8 SAUSAGE ROLLS • COST: £ £ £ £ £

INGREDIENTS:

- 8 sausages
- ½ tsp vegetable or olive oil
- ½ tbsp plain flour
- 1 x 320 g pack ready-made puff pastry
- 1 egg, beaten

INSTRUCTIONS:

1. Preheat the oven to 220°C.

2. Take the sausages out of the fridge.

3. Grease the baking tray with the oil. Sprinkle the greased surface with the flour and then bang the tray against the surface to dislodge some of the flour. Repeat. Once the tray has a fine dusting of flour on the oil, nothing will stick to it.

4. Unroll the pastry keeping it on its paper sheet. Cut it into eight pieces.

5. Put a sausage in the middle of each section of pastry.

6. Prepare the egg and use the pastry brush to brush one long side of the pastry.

7. Roll the pastry around the sausages, sealing the edges with the egg.

8. Place all sausage rolls in the baking tray, with gaps between.

9. Using the pastry brush, paint egg on top of each to ensure a golden finish.

10. Place in the centre of the oven and cook for 20 minutes, until cooked through.

11. Allow to cool for 5 minutes before serving.

TIP: You can cut these to make mini sausage rolls.

SALAD JARS

TIME NEEDED: 45 MINUTES •
SERVES: 4–8 (JARS CAN BE SHARED) • COST: £ £ £ £ £

INGREDIENTS:

For the salad:

- 2 carrots, grated
- 1 red pepper, deseeded and finely diced
- 2 celery stalks, finely diced
- 1–2 spring onions or ½ leek (white parts only), finely sliced
- 20 g fresh coriander, including stalks, chopped
- Optional: 2 tbsp toasted seeds (sesame seeds, pumpkin seeds, sunflower seeds, etc.)
- Optional: 30 g of your favourite nuts (peanuts, almonds, cashews, hazelnuts, walnuts, etc.)

For the dressing:

- 2 tbsp sesame oil
- 1 tbsp fresh squeezed lemon juice
- 1 tbsp honey or maple syrup
- 2 tsp soy sauce
- 1 tsp grated ginger
- 1 clove garlic, grated or minced
- Seasoning to taste (salt and pepper)

INSTRUCTIONS:

1. Layer the prepared vegetables into the jars in the order of your choice. When complete, put the lids on the jars and place in the fridge.

2. To make the dressing, put all the ingredients into a jar. Add the lid and shake to thoroughly combine.

3. To make toasted seeds, heat a frying pan over a medium heat for one minute (no oil) and add the seeds. Cook for about 2–3 minutes, until brown, stirring every minute or so. Do not overheat the pan or the seeds can explode. When cooked, remove from the heat.

4. When ready to complete the salad, remove the jar from the fridge, pour the dressing into the tops of the jars, sprinkle with the nuts and toasted seeds, if using, and serve or replace the lid until required.

BLACK BEAN QUESADILLAS

Mission brief

- **Kit**: Bowl, measuring scales and spoons, frying pan, spatula, chopping board and knife.
- **Skills**: Measuring, mixing, grating, chopping.
- **Mission notes**: I use these as an alternative to sandwiches and they always go down well. Even better, the filling can be made in advance and left in the fridge to chill until you're ready to fry them.

TIME NEEDED: 45 MINUTES • SERVES: 4–8 • COST: £ £ £ £ £

INGREDIENTS:

- 400 g can black beans, drained
- 2 spring onions, sliced, or ¼ red onion, finely chopped
- 1 red pepper, deseeded and chopped
- 80 g Cheddar cheese, grated
- ½ tsp ground cumin
- ½ tsp dried oregano
- Seasoning to taste (salt and pepper)
- 8 small tortilla wraps
- 1 tbsp cooking oil

INSTRUCTIONS:

1. Place the prepared black beans, spring onions, pepper and grated cheese into a large bowl and mix well.

2. Add the cumin and oregano, give it a good mix and season to taste.

3. If using later, cover and place in the fridge.

4. When ready, lay out the eight tortilla wraps.

5 Divide the filling between them, placing it on one half of the wrap only.

6 Take each wrap, fold in half, press down to squash all of the ingredients a little, and place on a plate.

7 Heat a little of the oil in a pan on a medium heat and add two of the quesadillas, pressing them down with the spatula to ensure the outside becomes brown and crunchy. Turn them over and repeat. Remove from the heat, add a little more oil and repeat until all quesadillas are cooked and serve.

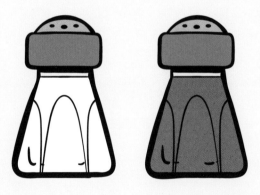

FALAFEL AND PITTA

Mission brief

- **Kit:** Garlic press (optional), chopping board and sharp knife, large frying pan, large mixing bowl, masher, spatula.
- **Skills:** Chopping, mashing, making falafel balls, toasting.

TIME NEEDED: 45 MINUTES • SERVES: 4 • COST: £££££

INGREDIENTS:

- 4 wholewheat pitta
- ¼ cucumber, chopped
- 8 cherry tomatoes, halved
- 4 leaves iceberg lettuce, shredded

For the falafel:

- 400 g can chickpeas, drained and washed
- 1 tsp ground cumin
- 1 tsp ground coriander
- 2 tbsp cooking oil
- 1 small onion, finely chopped
- 1 garlic clove, minced or grated
- 20 g coriander, including stalks, chopped
- 20 g parsley, including stalks, chopped
- 1 egg, beaten

INSTRUCTIONS:

1. Place the chickpeas, ground cumin and ground coriander in a bowl and set aside.

2. Heat 1 tbsp oil in the pan on a low heat, and gently fry the onion and garlic for 5 minutes until softened but not coloured.

③ Remove from the heat and add to the mixing bowl with the chickpeas, then mix everything together, mashing into a chunky paste with a potato masher.

④ Stir in the fresh herbs and the egg.

⑤ Using your hands form the mixture into eight falafel balls.

⑥ Heat 1 tbsp oil in the pan on a medium heat, then fry the falafels, pressing them down gently in the pan with the spatula to form patties.

⑦ Cook for 3 minutes on each side, until golden brown. Set aside.

⑧ Gently toast the pitta, and cut in half widthways to make pitta pockets.

⑨ To each pitta add one falafel patty, shredded lettuce, cucumber and tomato and serve.

TIP: You can toast the pitta in your toaster. Place them in the toaster uncut and turn them around after a minute or two to ensure both ends are toasted. Then take them out and cut in half – just be careful, as the air inside is very hot.

SQUASHED PICNIC SANDWICH

Mission brief

- **Kit:** Cling film or beeswax wraps, chopping board and knife, measuring spoons.
- **Skills:** Cutting, measuring, wrapping.
- **Mission notes:** This is perfect for a picnic: A large ciabatta, packed full of ingredients that are squashed together to make a really tasty sandwich. Even better if made the night before the picnic.

TIME NEEDED: 30 MINUTES • SERVES: 8 • COST: £ £ £ £ £

INGREDIENTS:

- Ciabatta baguette – sliced in half lengthways
- Butter, for spreading
- 2 handfuls of baby spinach or watercress, washed
- 12 slices of salami
- 2 balls of mozzarella, sliced
- 1 yellow pepper, deseeded and sliced
- 3 tomatoes, sliced
- 3 tbsp basil pesto

INSTRUCTIONS:

1 Butter the ciabatta baguette

2 Assemble the sandwich in layers: start with the spinach, then salami, mozzarella, pepper, tomatoes.

③ Spread the pesto on the top half of the loaf and sandwich the two halves together.

④ Wrap tightly in cling film or beeswax wraps and put it in the fridge with something heavy on top.

⑤ To serve, take to your picnic and slice as thinly or thickly as you wish! Enjoy!

TIP: Swap out any ingredients you don't like.

BENTO BOX LUNCHES

Mission brief

- **Mission notes:** A bento box is a small meal made up of several different elements. Using this idea, you can put together some tasty, interesting packed lunches that the troopers will love – and all take less than 15 minutes to put together. Don't forget to pack the water bottle.

BENTO BOX 1 – MARGARITA PIZZA

- Cheddar cheese, cut into sticks
- Pepperoni slices
- Cherry tomatoes
- Crackers
- Grapes

BENTO BOX 2 – GREEK SALAD

- Portion of hummus
- Toasted pitta bread, cut into fingers
- Sliced carrots, peppers and celery for dipping
- Cubes of cheese (it doesn't have to be feta, just use your trooper's favourite)
- Grapes

BENTO BOX 3 – CHICKEN TACO

- Portion of leftover chicken (or any other meat you have)
- Tortilla chips
- Cherry tomatoes
- Strawberries
- Shredded iceberg lettuce

BENTO BOX 4 – OMELETTE

- 2 boiled eggs, halved
- Cubes of cheese
- Slices of pepper
- Small handful of almonds
- Banana (if you're using a portion of a large banana, leave the skin on to prevent the flesh browning)

BENTO BOX 5 – PB&J BENTO BOX

- Peanut butter sandwich on wholemeal, cut into 4
- Celery chunks
- Blueberries and strawberries
- Yoghurt

HUMMUS AND VEGETABLES

Mission brief
- **Kit:** Chopping board and knife, food processor, measuring spoons, juicer.
- **Skills:** Chopping, using a food processor, juicing.

TIME NEEDED: 30 MINUTES • SERVES: 8 • COST: £ £ £ £ £

INGREDIENTS:

- Suitable raw vegetables; they must be juicy but firm enough for dipping. Good choices include, but are not limited to, carrots, peppers, baby corn, mangetout, cauliflower and broccoli. Chop them to roughly equal sizes, suitable for your troopers to hold.
- 400 g can chickpeas, drained
- 1 tbsp tahini paste (you can use Greek yoghurt or peanut butter as alternatives)
- ¼ tsp ground cumin
- 1 tbsp olive oil
- Juice of ½ lemon
- 2 tbsp water

INSTRUCTIONS:

1. Arrange the chopped vegetables on a large plate.
2. Put chickpeas, tahini paste, cumin and olive oil into the food processor and blitz to form a paste.
3. While the food processor is running, slowly add the lemon juice and water until the hummus has reached the desired consistency. If still too stiff, add more water.
4. To serve, spoon into individual bowls and let troopers help themselves to vegetables.

TREATS

This section has recipes for mouth-watering treats that are easy to make and oh-so-easy to eat. Of course, a "treat" should be enjoyed in moderation – if you're having them all the time, they're not treats. But there's no doubt a little bit of what you fancy does you good!

TIFFIN

Mission brief

- **Kit:** 18-cm square baking tin, non-stick baking parchment or greaseproof paper, large mixing bowl, large heatproof bowl, small saucepan, plastic bag for smashing biscuits, rolling pin, silicone spoon or spatula, oven gloves.
- **Skills:** Using a bain-marie, crushing biscuits, stirring, lining.

TIME NEEDED: 1 HOUR • MAKES: 16 PIECES (A LITTLE GOES A LONG WAY!) • COST: £ £ £ £ £

INGREDIENTS:

- 300 g digestive biscuits, crushed
- 170 g dark chocolate, broken into pieces
- 115 g unsalted butter, plus extra for greasing
- 397 g can condensed milk
- 30 g raisins
- 170 g milk chocolate, broken into pieces

INSTRUCTIONS:

1. Grease baking tin with a little butter, then line with parchment.

2. Prepare the biscuits by placing in a large plastic bag and crushing with a rolling pin. Tip into a large mixing bowl.

3. Place the heatproof bowl over a pan of gently boiling water – the edge of the bowl must be wider than the pan to form a seal. This is known as a bain-marie and is a method to melt things gently, so keep the water simmering.

④ Add dark chocolate, butter and condensed milk to the bowl and allow to melt together, then stir ingredients to form a smooth, shiny liquid.

⑤ Remove bowl (carefully!) and pour the mixture onto the biscuits. Scrape the bowl clean with your silicone spatula (as you will later use it to melt your milk chocolate).

⑥ Add the raisins to the biscuit mixture and stir well.

⑦ Pour into the lined tray and spread out evenly and leave to cool.

⑧ Add the milk chocolate to the bain-marie and melt gently.

⑨ Pour the melted milk chocolate over the mix.

⑩ Chill until set, about 1–2 hours, and serve.

TIP: Best stored in the fridge – but find a good place to hide it!

BANANA BREAD

Mission brief

- **Kit:** A 20 cm x 12.5 cm loaf tin, large mixing bowl, sieve, wooden spoon.
- **Skills:** Greasing, beating, mashing, stirring, sifting, folding.
- **Mission notes:** A great way to use up overripe bananas.

**TIME NEEDED: 1 HOUR 30 MINUTES • SERVES: 8 •
COST: £ £ £ £ £**

INGREDIENTS:

- 110 g unsalted butter, at room temperature, plus extra for greasing
- 225 g caster sugar
- 2 eggs
- 4 small ripe or overripe bananas, mashed
- 90 ml milk
- 1 tsp vanilla extract
- 275 g plain flour
- 1 tsp bicarbonate of soda

INSTRUCTIONS:

1. Preheat the oven to 180°C.

2. Grease the loaf tin.

3. In a large mixing bowl, beat together the butter and sugar until light, fluffy and pale.

4. Beat the eggs and stir into the mixture.

5. Stir in the mashed bananas, milk and vanilla extract. Mix well.

6 Sift in the flour and bicarbonate of soda and fold into the banana mixture until combined.

7 Transfer the mixture to the loaf tin and bake for 55–60 minutes, or until golden brown, and serve.

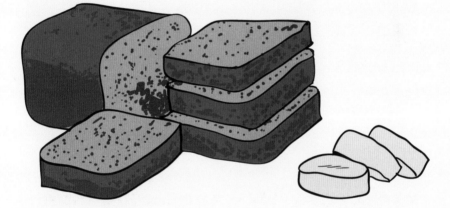

CARROT CAKE

Mission brief

- **Kit:** 23-cm cake tin, sieve, large mixing bowl, small bowl, wire rack, measuring scales, jug and spoons, palette knife.
- **Skills:** Sifting, measuring, mixing.

TIME NEEDED: 1 HOUR 45 MINUTES • MAKES: 12 SLICES • COST: £ £ £ £ £

INGREDIENTS:

For the cake:

- 200 g plain flour
- 2 tsp baking powder
- 1 tsp salt
- 1 tsp bicarbonate of soda
- 200 g brown sugar
- 250 g carrots, grated
- Optional: 110 g walnuts
- 150 ml vegetable oil, plus extra for greasing
- 2 eggs, beaten

For the icing:

- 110 g unsalted butter
- 225 g cream cheese
- 50 g icing sugar
- 1 tsp vanilla extract

INSTRUCTIONS:

1. Preheat the oven to 160°C.
2. Grease the cake tin.
3. In a large bowl, sift the flour, baking powder, salt and bicarbonate of soda together. Stir well.

4 Add the sugar, prepared carrots, walnuts if using, oil and beaten eggs, and stir until combined.

5 Transfer to the tin and bake for 65–70 minutes.

6 Place on a wire rack and allow to cool before removing from the cake tin.

7 In a small bowl, beat together the butter and cream cheese until light and fluffy.

8 Add the sugar and vanilla extract and stir well.

9 Make sure the cake is cold before spreading the icing over it using a palette knife, and serve.

CHOCOLATE BROWNIES

Mission brief

- **Kit:** 18-cm square cake tin, non-stick baking parchment or greaseproof paper, small saucepan, heatproof bowl, electric blender or whisk.
- **Skills:** Greasing, whisking, beating, melting in a bain-marie.

TIME NEEDED: 1 HOUR 30 MINUTES •
MAKES: 16 BROWNIES • COST: £ £ £ £ £

INGREDIENTS:

- 200 g dark chocolate
- 150 g unsalted butter, plus extra for greasing
- 2 eggs
- 200 g dark muscovado sugar
- 100 g plain flour
- 1 tsp baking powder

INSTRUCTIONS:

1. Preheat oven to 160°C.

2. Grease the cake tin and line with parchment or greaseproof paper.

3. Bring half a saucepan of water to a gentle boil.

4. Place the heatproof bowl in the pan – the edge of the bowl must be wider than the pan to form a seal.

5. Place the chocolate and butter in the bowl to melt, then stir to combine.

6. Beat the eggs and sugar together in a separate bowl using a handheld mixer or whisk.

7 Add the melted chocolate and butter to the egg mixture and stir.

8 Add the flour and baking powder and stir thoroughly.

9 Pour the mixture into the tin and place in the oven.

10 Bake for 30 minutes.

11 Allow to cool for 10 minutes before cutting into 16 squares, and serve.

FLAPJACKS

Mission brief

- **Kit:** 20-cm square baking tin, non-stick baking parchment or greaseproof paper, small saucepan, wooden spoon, measuring scales.
- **Skills:** Greasing, melting, measuring, stirring.

TIME NEEDED: 1 HOUR 15 MINUTES •
MAKES: 16 FLAPJACKS • COST: £ £ £ £ £

INGREDIENTS:

- 175 g unsalted butter, plus extra for greasing
- 175 g muscovado sugar
- 175 g golden syrup
- 340 g porridge oats

INSTRUCTIONS:

1. Preheat the oven to 150°C.

2. Grease the baking tin and line with the greaseproof paper.

3. Melt the butter in a small pan over a low heat.

4. Gradually add the sugar and syrup and stir until the sugar is dissolved.

5. Remove from the heat, add in the porridge oats and mix well.

6. Tip the mixture into the baking tin and use a wooden spoon to flatten.

7. Bake for 40 minutes.

8. Allow to cool before cutting into 16 squares or slices, and serve.

AVOCADO CHOCOLATE MOUSSE

Mission brief

- **Kit:** Chopping board and knife, hand blender.
- **Skills:** Blending, stoning an avocado.

TIME NEEDED: 15 MINUTES • SERVES: 4 • COST: £££££

INGREDIENTS:

- 2 small ripe avocados, halved and stoned
- 1 tbsp unsweetened cocoa powder
- 1 generous tbsp runny honey
- 1 tbsp cold water

INSTRUCTIONS:

1. Spoon the flesh from the prepared avocados into a bowl.

2. Add the cocoa, honey and water.

3. Blend with a hand blender until smooth.

4. Chill until you're ready to serve.

MILLIONAIRE SHORTBREAD

Mission brief
- **Kit:** 20-cm square cake tin, non-stick baking parchment or greaseproof paper, large mixing bowl, measuring scales and spoons.
- **Skills:** Greasing, rubbing, measuring.

TIME NEEDED: 1 HOUR 45 MINUTES • MAKES: 16 SQUARES • COST: £ £ £ £ £

INGREDIENTS:

For the shortbread:
- 175 g unsalted butter, kept cold and chopped into cubes, plus extra for greasing
- 225 g plain flour
- 75 g caster sugar
- 2 tsp vanilla essence

For the caramel:
- 200 g unsalted butter
- 400 g can condensed milk
- 4 tbsp golden syrup
- 1 tsp salt

For the topping:
- 340 g milk chocolate, broken into squares

INSTRUCTIONS:

1. Preheat the oven to 180°C.

2. Grease the cake tin and line with baking paper.

3. Sieve the flour into the mixing bowl.

4 Add the cold butter and rub until it looks like breadcrumbs.

5 Add the sugar and vanilla essence. Stir well to form a dough.

6 Transfer dough to the cake tin and press down to compact.

7 Bake for 40 minutes, reducing the heat of the oven to 150°C after 10 minutes.

8 Allow to cool in the tin.

9 In a large saucepan, bring the butter, condensed milk, syrup and salt to the boil and simmer for 10 minutes.

10 Pour the mixture over the shortbread, then chill in the fridge for 30 minutes until hardened.

11 Bring half a saucepan of water to a gentle boil.

12 Place the heatproof bowl in the pan – the edge of the bowl must be wider than the pan to form a seal.

13 Add the chocolate and melt, stirring.

14 Pour the chocolate over the caramel and chill in the fridge for 30 minutes, or until set.

15 Cut into squares and serve.

TIP: For guidance on how to "rub" flour and butter, go to page 60.

MICROWAVE TREACLE (OR JAM) SPONGE

SERVE WITH: Custard.

Mission brief

- **Kit:** 1-litre microwaveable bowl, plate large enough to act as a lid, zester or grater, mixing bowl, hand blender or whisk, measuring scales and spoons.
- **Skills:** Zesting, blending or whisking, measuring, beating.

TIME NEEDED: 30 MINUTES • SERVES: 4 • COST: £ £ £ £ £

INGREDIENTS:

- 125 g unsalted butter, plus extra for greasing
- 3 tbsp golden syrup or your favourite jam
- 100 g caster sugar
- 2 eggs
- 125 g self-raising flour

- 1 tbsp whole milk
- Zest of 1 lemon. The zest is the bright yellow part of the skin – avoid the white part which is bitter – and can be removed with a zester or, if you don't have one, the fine side of your grater

INSTRUCTIONS:

1. Grease the bowl.

2. Spoon the syrup or jam into the bottom of the bowl and set aside.

3. In the mixing bowl, beat the butter and sugar until smooth, fluffy and pale.

4 Beat the eggs into the mixture, one at a time until fully combined.

5 Fold in the flour, then mix in the milk and lemon zest.

6 Spoon the mixture into the microwavable bowl, cover with a plate and microwave on full power for 5 minutes.

7 Leave to stand for 3–4 minutes.

8 Turn out onto a plate and serve.

JAM TARTS

Mission brief

- **Kit:** 12–16-hole tart tray, cookie cutter, measuring scales and spoons, mixing bowl, rolling pin, cling film.
- **Skills:** Measuring, mixing, greasing, rolling dough, separating egg yolk from egg white.

TIME NEEDED: 1 HOUR • MAKES: 12–16 TARTS • COST: £ £ £ £ £

INGREDIENTS:

- 75 g unsalted butter, kept cold and chopped into cubes, plus extra for greasing
- 150 g plain flour
- Pinch of salt
- 50 g caster sugar
- 1 egg yolk
- 1 tbsp cold water
- Jam of your choice

INSTRUCTIONS:

1. Preheat the oven to 190°C.

2. Grease the tart tray.

3. Sieve the flour and salt into the mixing bowl.

4. Add the cold butter and rub until it looks like breadcrumbs.

5. Add the sugar and separated egg yolk, and stir well to form a dough (add water, if necessary).

6. Knead the dough gently, then wrap in cling film. Chill in the fridge for 15 minutes.

7. Dust your work surface lightly with flour.

8. Roll out the pastry to a ½ cm thickness.

9. Using a cookie cutter, cut into rounds slightly bigger than the holes in the tray. Press one into each hole.

10. Put 1–2 tsp jam into each pastry case, making sure they are not overfilled.

11. You can use any extra pastry to make decorations for your tarts (initials are popular).

12. Bake for 15–18 minutes, or until golden brown, and leave to cool before serving.

TIP: Jam expands when hot so be careful not to add too much.

TIP: For guidance on how to "rub" flour and butter, go to page 60.

GINGERBREAD PEOPLE

Mission brief

- **Kit:** Baking tray, non-stick baking parchment or greaseproof paper, two mixing bowls, measuring spoons, rolling pin, cling film, gingerbread person cutter.
- **Skills:** Beating, measuring, kneading, rolling.

**TIME NEEDED: 1 HOUR 30 MINUTES •
MAKES: APPROX. 12 BISCUITS • COST: £ £ £ £ £**

INGREDIENTS:

- 110 g unsalted butter, plus extra for greasing
- 340 g plain flour
- 1 tsp bicarbonate of soda
- 1 tsp ground cinnamon
- 2½ tsp ground ginger
- 175 g light brown sugar
- 1 egg
- 4 tbsp golden syrup

INSTRUCTIONS:

1. Preheat the oven to 180°C.

2. Grease tray with a little butter, then line the baking tray with paper.

3. In the first mixing bowl:
   - Sift the flour, add the bicarbonate of soda, cinnamon and ginger, and stir.
   - Add the butter and sugar, and beat.

4. In the second mixing bowl:

   - Beat the egg with the golden syrup. Add this to the mixture in the first bowl and stir until it forms a dough.

5. Dust your work surface lightly with flour.

6. Knead the dough until smooth, wrap in cling film and chill in the fridge for 20 minutes.

7. When ready, lightly dust the work surface with flour.

8. Roll out the dough and cut out the people with a cutter.

9. Place them on the baking tray, leaving about 5 cm between each biscuit – they spread out!

10. Bake for 15 minutes, or until golden brown, and serve.

TIP: For guidance on how to knead dough, go to page 42.

CHEESECAKE

SERVE WITH: Fresh fruit.

Mission brief

- **Kit:** Large sandwich or food storage bag and rolling pin for crushing the biscuits, two mixing bowls, small saucepan, 20-cm flan tin or springform cake tin (the bottom and sides can be removed).
- **Skills:** Greasing, measuring, whipping.

TIME NEEDED: 1 HOUR • SERVES: 6 • COST: £ £ £ £ £

INGREDIENTS:

- 75 g unsalted butter, plus extra for greasing
- 175 g digestive biscuits
- 225 g cream cheese
- 175 g condensed milk
- 150 ml double cream

INSTRUCTIONS:

1. Grease the flan or cake tin.

2. Prepare the biscuits by putting them in the bag and gently crushing with a rolling pin.

3. Melt butter in the pan, then add the crushed biscuits and mix thoroughly.

4. Pour the biscuit mixture into the tin, pressing it down firmly to create an even base layer and chill in a fridge for 10 minutes.

5. Mix the cream cheese and condensed milk in a bowl.

6 In the clean mixing bowl, whip the cream until it begins to stiffen (being careful not to over whisk).

7 Fold in the cream cheese mixture.

8 Spoon the mixture on top of the chilled biscuit base.

9 Return to the fridge for at least 30 minutes before serving.

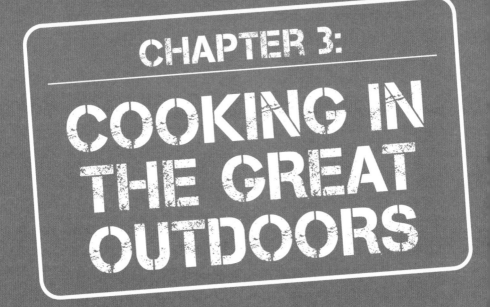

CHAPTER 3:
COOKING IN THE GREAT OUTDOORS

BUILDING A FIRE

If you're planning to cook in the great outdoors – even if it is your garden at base camp – you'll first need to know how to choose a safe area to build your fire, how to build an effective fire to cook on, and very importantly, how to safely put it out.

Mission brief

- Kit:
  - Fire safety equipment: First aid kit; full bucket of water (for fire safety and putting out the fire); fireproof gloves.
  - An ignition source: Matches or a lighter are a great place to start. Advanced methods include flint and steel, a fire steel or friction.
  - Rocks to enclose your fire circle.
  - A garden trowel to dig a fire pit (if not using stones).
  - Tinder: To catch the initial spark from the ignition source and transfer it to the kindling. If the kindling is damp or wet, the tinder must burn long enough to dry out the kindling. Good sources: Dead dry plants and grasses, wood shavings, cotton wool.
  - Kindling: Needs more bulk than tinder so it can ignite easily, produce sustained heat and flame, and light the main fuel source. Good sources: Dry twigs and wood pieces and cardboard.
  - Bulky fuel sources for sustained burning. Good sources include dry wood that is 3–12 cm in diameter, peat, dried animal dung and coal.
- **Skills:** Making a fire pit or a stone fire circle; setting and lighting a campfire; safely maintaining a campfire; effectively putting out a campfire.

- **Mission notes:** Here are a few things you must consider when choosing an area to build your fire:
  - If you're in your own garden, choose an area away from any trees and bushes you may have. If you are on someone else's land, check with the landowner if they allow fires before you go ahead.
  - Look overhead – make sure there are no overhanging branches.
  - If you don't have a fire pit, you should build a fire circle out of stones, to help contain the ash and embers, and to keep people a safe distance away from the fire.
  - Keep firewood away from fire area until ready to use.

TIME NEEDED: ANYWHERE BETWEEN 30 MINUTES AND SEVERAL HOURS!

INSTRUCTIONS:

1 Clear a circular area about 1.2 metres in diameter (the "fire circle").

2 Build a ring of rocks around the fire circle to insulate the fire (alternatively, dig a fire pit around 10 cm deep with a small garden trowel).

3 Pile the trooper-collected kindling loosely in your fire ring or fire pit. The kindling needs to be dense enough to light but spaced out enough to enable air to circulate (fire needs oxygen to burn).

4 Place the tinder that your trooper has collected on the pile of kindling. Light the tinder with your ignition source and gradually add more kindling.

5 Slowly blow air on the igniting fire to build heat and intensity.

6 When your kindling has "caught", and is burning well, start adding firewood. Start with the smallest sized pieces and work your way up to larger pieces.

7 The arrangement of the firewood determines the fire's longevity, how fast it burns, and how long it lasts. The most effective arrangement is the tepee.

Making a tepee fire

1 Arrange the tinder and a few sticks of kindling in the shape of a cone.

2 Stick four kindling twigs in the ground to form a tepee above the tinder.

3 Leave an opening for you to light the fire, ideally on the upwind side to ensure any flame will blow up and toward the wood.

4 Build up the rest of the tepee, from small kindling twigs to larger twigs to logs, making sure there is room for air to circulate.

5 Light the tinder at the centre.

 As the flames become established the outside logs will fall inward and feed the fire.

⚠ WARNING

Please exercise caution, common sense and close supervision throughout every stage of this exercise. Make sure your troopers know how to behave and stay safe before you begin. It might be a good idea to practise in the garden back at base camp before venturing out and about.

PUTTING A FIRE OUT SAFELY

If you want to leave the site before the fire has burned out naturally, you will need to put it out and return the area to as close to how you found it as possible. A Commando Dad adopts a "leave no trace" attitude when doing any activity in the great outdoors.

Mission brief
- **Kit:** Water, trowel, fireproof gloves.
- **Skills:** Putting out a fire safely.

INSTRUCTIONS:

1. Spread out the burning embers, moving them away from each other using your trowel or a stick.

2. Soak the whole area where the fire has been with plenty of water.

3. When there is no smoke, the fire is out.

All the following recipes require hot coals – the flames are no longer on the fire but the coals or wooden embers are burning red.

ORANGE COUSCOUS

Mission brief

- **Kit:** Kitchen foil, fireproof gloves, chopping board and knife, spoons, hot embers.
- **Skills:** Cutting, scooping, wrapping in foil.
- **Mission notes:** This recipe involves using scooped-out oranges – keep the flesh for use in smoothies. The couscous makes a lovely, moist orangey accompaniment to the other recipes.

TIME NEEDED: 30 MINUTES • SERVES: 4 • COST: £ £ £ £ £

INGREDIENTS:

- 4 large oranges
- Boiling water (take a Thermos or a camping kettle if you are away from base camp)
- 110 g packet of couscous
- Optional: Handful sultanas

INSTRUCTIONS:

1. Cut the tops off the oranges and set aside.

2. Carefully scoop out the flesh of the orange, taking care to keep the skin of the orange intact. You don't have to remove all the flesh perfectly.

3. If you are at base camp, you can use your kettle for boiling water. If you are out and about, you can take a Thermos or use a camping kettle for your water – just make sure you *always* use your fireproof gloves when removing the kettle from the fire embers.

4. Quarter fill each orange with couscous and add a few sultanas if using, then wrap in foil, leaving the top open.

5. Pour boiling water over the couscous until it is about 1 cm above its surface.

6. Put the lid back on, then gather up the foil at the top, so it looks like a Christmas bauble. This will act as a "handle" to help you pull it out of the fire.

7. Wait 5–10 minutes for the couscous to soften and cook – then remove from the fire and carefully unwrap the foil, and serve.

8. Enjoy as an accompaniment to any of the other recipes you cook while in the great outdoors!

LEMON CAKE SERVED IN A LEMON

Mission brief

- **Kit:** Kitchen foil, chopping board and knife, measuring scales, mixing bowl, spoon, fireproof gloves, hot embers.
- **Skills:** Cutting, scooping, mixing, wrapping in foil, measuring.
- **Mission notes:** Being a Commando Dad is all about preparation and planning, so you can pre-prepare the ingredients at base camp and transport them to your outdoor fire area if you wish. This recipe makes little tangy sponge cakes, again using the skins of a fruit. Reserve the lemon flesh for use in another recipe.

TIME NEEDED: 40 MINUTES • SERVES: 6 • COST: £ £ £ £ £

INGREDIENTS:

- 6 lemons
- 50 g butter, room temperature
- 50 g brown sugar
- 50 g self-raising flour
- 1 egg

INSTRUCTIONS:

1. Cut the tops off the lemons, squeeze the juice from the lid, and set aside.

2. Carefully scoop out the flesh of the lemon, taking care to keep the skin of the lemon intact. You don't have to remove all the flesh perfectly.

3. Place the butter, sugar and flour into the mixing bowl and give it a thorough mix.

4 Add the egg and some lemon juice and mix.

5 Spoon this mix into the six lemons, filling about halfway (do not overfill).

6 Place the lid back on top and double wrap in foil, gathering it up at the top, so it looks like a Christmas bauble. This will act as a "handle" to help you pull it out of the fire.

7 Nestle each lemon bauble in the coals for about 20 minutes until they are cooked through, and serve.

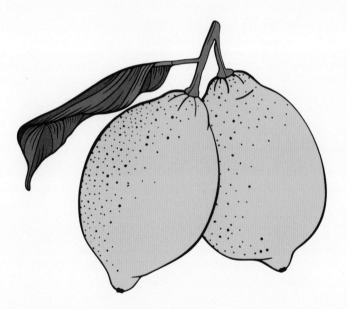

CAMPFIRE JACKET POTATOES

Mission brief

- **Kit:** Kitchen foil, fireproof gloves, hot embers.
- **Skills:** Wrapping in foil.
- **Mission notes:** Being a Commando Dad is all about preparation and planning, so you can pre-prepare your potatoes at base camp and transport them to your outdoor fire area if you wish.

TIME NEEDED: 70 MINUTES (POTATOES CAN TAKE ABOUT AN HOUR, DEPENDING ON THEIR SIZE) • SERVES: 4 • COST: £ £ £ £ £

INGREDIENTS:

- 4 baking potatoes, cleaned
- 4 tbsp of butter
- Filling (such as butter, grated cheese, beans, coleslaw)

INSTRUCTIONS:

1. Pierce every potato all over with a fork before smearing with 1 tablespoon of butter.

2. Double-wrap potatoes in kitchen foil.

3. Bury the potatoes in the hot coals.

4. Allow to cook for 30 to 60 minutes until soft.

5. Carefully unwrap each potato, slice open and serve with the filling of your choice.

CAMPFIRE PIZZA

Mission brief

- **Kit:** Sharp knife, fireproof gloves, cast iron pan, spatula.
- **Skills:** Chopping.

TIME NEEDED: 40 MINUTES • SERVES: 4 • COST: £ £ £ £ £

INGREDIENTS:

- 1 roll ready-made pizza dough
- 1 tbsp cooking oil
- 1–2 tbsp tomato purée
- Additional topping of your choice, such as pepperoni, mushrooms, and/or vegetables, sliced finely
- 100 g mozzarella (or your favourite cheese)

INSTRUCTIONS:

1. Measure your pizza dough – it needs to be no bigger than the base of your pan. Trim excess and set aside.
2. Rest your pan on the glowing embers for 5–10 minutes (until you cannot comfortably hold the back of your hand a few centimetres above the pan) and add your oil.
3. Place your pizza dough into the pan.
4. Cook until the bottom has browned.
5. Wearing the fireproof gloves, remove the pan from the fire and flip the crust in the pan.
6. Spread with tomato purée, add your other toppings, if using, then the cheese.
7. Return to the heat and cook until the toppings are warmed through and the cheese has melted, then serve.

COMMANDO NACHOS

> **Mission brief**
> - **Kit:** Cast iron pan with lid, bowl, grater, measuring spoons and scales, fireproof gloves, hot embers.
> - **Skills:** Measuring, cutting, grating.

TIME NEEDED: 40 MINUTES • SERVES: 4 • COST: £ £ £ £ £

INGREDIENTS:

- 1 tbsp cooking oil
- 2 spring onions, finely sliced
- 1 red pepper, deseeded and chopped
- 1 yellow pepper, deseeded and chopped
- 1 tomato, roughly chopped
- 1 bag tortilla chips
- Optional: Jar of salsa
- 50 g cheese, grated

INSTRUCTIONS:

1. Rest your pan on the glowing embers for 5–10 minutes (until you cannot comfortably hold your hand a few centimetres above the pan) and add your oil.

2. Fry onions, peppers and tomato for 5 minutes then place in the bowl.

3. Add tortilla chips to pan, then add salsa (if using), the onion and pepper mix and, finally, the cheese.

4. Place lid on and allow to cook for 15 minutes, checking regularly, and then serve.

SAUSAGE AND BEAN ONE-POT WONDER

Mission brief

- **Kit:** Cast iron pan, spoon, garlic press (optional), chopping board and sharp knife, measuring spoons, colander or sieve, spatula, fireproof gloves, hot embers.
- **Skills:** Chopping, measuring, stirring.

TIME NEEDED: 45 MINUTES • SERVES: 4 • COST: £ £ £ £ £

INGREDIENTS:

- 1 tbsp cooking oil
- 8 pork sausages
- 1 garlic clove, chopped or minced
- 1 leek, trimmed and thinly sliced
- 1 carrot, roughly chopped
- 200 ml beef stock (1 stock cube)
- 400 g can chopped tomatoes
- 2 x 400 g cans cannellini beans, drained and rinsed

INSTRUCTIONS:

1. Rest your pan on the glowing embers for 5–10 minutes (until you cannot comfortably hold your hand a few centimetres above the pan) and add half your oil.

2. Add the sausages and brown for 5 minutes, turning regularly. Remove and set aside.

3. Using the rest of the oil, fry the garlic, leek and carrot for 10 minutes.

4. Add the stock, tomatoes and sausages and cook for 10 minutes.

5. Stir in the beans and allow to simmer for 3–5 minutes to warm the beans through and serve.

BARBECUED BANANA WITH CHOCOLATE CHUNKS

Mission brief

- **Kit:** Sharp knife, kitchen foil, fireproof gloves, hot embers.
- **Skills:** Cutting, wrapping in foil.

TIME NEEDED: 40 MINUTES • SERVES: 4 • COST: £ £ £ £ £

INGREDIENTS:

- Small bar milk chocolate
- 4 bananas

INSTRUCTIONS:

1. Break the chocolate into small pieces.

2. Do not peel the banana, instead, pierce the skin into the flesh, and cut a slit along the length of the banana.

3. Gently open the slit and place the chocolate chunks into the banana flesh.

4. Wrap the banana tightly in the foil and place directly onto the embers for about 20 minutes.

5. Carefully remove the foil parcel from the coals and leave to cool for a few minutes. To serve, simply open the foil and eat the flesh from within the skin.

FIRE BREAD

Mission brief

- **Kit:** Bowl, fireproof gloves, fire sticks (1 metre in length) – just clean sticks you can wrap your dough around.
- **Skills:** Cutting, kneading, wrapping, toasting.

TIME NEEDED: 40 MINUTES • SERVES: 4 • COST: £ £ £ £ £

INGREDIENTS:

- 175 g self-raising flour
- A few splashes of water

INSTRUCTIONS:

1. Mix together the flour with a few splashes of water. You need a dough that holds together, but doesn't stick to your hands. If it's like breadcrumbs, add a little more water – if it's too gooey, add a little more flour.

2. Divide the dough into four tennis-ball-sized balls, and roll them into long sausage shapes.

3. Twist the dough sausages around your fire sticks.

4. Hold the sticks over the embers for 10–15 minutes, turning them to ensure an even cook.

5. When the bread is cooked, it will sound hollow when you tap it.

6. Eat as is, with butter, or as an accompaniment to another fiery recipe.

S'MORES

Mission brief

- **Kit:** Four wooden skewers (soaked in water for 30 minutes first so that they don't catch fire), fireproof gloves.
- **Skills:** Toasting.

TIME NEEDED: 10 MINUTES • SERVES: 4 • COST: £ £ £ £ £

INGREDIENTS:

- 8 big marshmallows
- 8 chocolate digestive biscuits

INSTRUCTIONS:

1. Place a marshmallow onto the end of a wooden skewer, making sure the skewer is long enough so that you or your troopers can stay a safe distance from the fire.

2. Hold over the embers, and keep turning the skewer, until the marshmallow is toasted and gooey. Blow on it for 30 seconds.

3. Place the melted marshmallow between two chocolate digestives, chocolate sides touching the marshmallow.

4. Squash together and enjoy.

FIERY CAMPFIRE VEG

Mission brief

- **Kit:** Chopping board and a knife, cast iron pan with lid, fireproof gloves.
- **Skills:** Cutting.

TIME NEEDED: 30 MINUTES • SERVES: 4 • COST: £ £ £ £ £

INGREDIENTS:

- 1 courgette, sliced
- 3 corn on the cob, cut into thirds (9 small corn cobs)
- 2 peppers, deseeded and chopped
- 1 medium onion, chopped
- 1 tbsp cooking oil
- ½ tbsp paprika

INSTRUCTIONS:

1. Rest your pan on the glowing embers for 5–10 minutes (until you cannot comfortably hold the back of your hand a few centimetres above the pan).

2. Place all prepared veg into the pan and drizzle with your oil.

3. Sprinkle the paprika over and give everything a good stir.

4. Put the lid on and allow to cook for 15 minutes, stirring occasionally.

5. Plate up with any of the other campfire food you've prepared, then enjoy!

INDEX

RECIPES

Basic Recipes

Breakfasts

Classics

NEIL SINCLAIR

COMMANDO DAD
BASIC TRAINING

HOW TO BE AN ELITE DAD OR CARER

THE BASICS

- Survive the first 24 hours
- Prepare and plan to prevent poor parental performance
- Maintain morale
- Feed, clothe, transport and entertain your troops

FROM BIRTH TO 3 YEARS

COMMANDO DAD

Foreword by Dr Jan Mager-Jones MB ChB